THE HANDBOOK FOR BEACH STROLLERS
FROM MAINE TO CAPE HATTERAS

"Read Nature not books.
If you study Nature in books,
when you go out-of-doors
you cannot find her."
—*Louis Agassiz*

THE HANDBOOK
FOR BEACH STROLLERS
FROM MAINE
TO CAPE HATTERAS
Second Edition

by
Donald Zinn

Illustrations by
Richard C. Grosvenor
Photography by R. S. Mackenzie

Chester, Connecticut

The original edition of *The Beach Strollers Handbook* was made up of 35 short articles, written as contributions to *Maritimes*, the quarterly publication of the University of Rhode Island's Graduate School of Oceanography. It was published in book form as Marine Bulletin Number 12 by the University of Rhode Island in 1973.

Library of Congress Cataloging in Publication Data
Zinn, Donald J. (Donald Joseph)
 The handbook for beach strollers from Maine to Cape Hatteras.

 Rev. ed. of: The beach strollers handbook, from Maine to Cape Hatteras. Rev. 1975.
 Includes index.
 1. Marine fauna—Atlantic Coast (U.S.)
2. Interstitial fauna—Atlantic Coast (U.S.)
3. Seashore biology—Atlantic Coast (U.S) I. Zinn, Donald J. (Donald Joseph). The Beach strollers handbook, from Maine to Cape Hatteras. II. Title.

QL127.Z56 1985   591.92′14   85-8156
ISBN 0-87106-871-0 (pbk.)

Manufactured in the United States of America
Second Edition/Second Printing

Contents

for Eleanor

Foreword to the First Edition

*F*or at least two generations, elementary and secondary public schools and most institutions of higher learning nurtured the myth that through science humanity could solve all its problems. Most of us over thirty were educated to believe that technology need only have enough attention and homage and, through it, humanity would sooner or later emerge supreme over all physical and biological earthly constraints.

We were led to believe that the best-educated of us was the technician who knew the most about the least—whose horizons were narrowest but most penetrating—who could speak of that subject only to researchers, and not even to them if we were really the best in our line. Because the fashionable sciences were biochemistry, molecular biology, biophysics, cytology, nuclear physics, physical engineering, and similar inward-peering disciplines, whole curricula were revised to allow entire faculties of teacher-researchers (a contradiction in temperaments, it seems to me) to inflict their interests on a generation or more of hapless high school and college students.

For most of us, science—biology in particular—came to mean hour upon hour of deadly lectures on aspects of life which were meaningless without an enthusiasm, an understanding, even a reverence for the commonplace inhabitants of the garden, pond, shore, or woods.

For those who, like myself, found unending fascination in living things (as opposed to formalin-soaked corpses), biology was one of the great disappointments. Learning to recognize life in the field was frowned on as "outdated." "It has all been done before," we were told. The pleasure of knowing where and how to find a particular animal or plant, understanding its behavioral characteristics, its food or its sex life, was looked on as frivolous since it made no contribution to extending the bounds of total knowledge. To be a respectable biologist, one had to be "research oriented." The animal itself, its community, and its relationship to that community, were not worthy of the attention of a biologist.

At the time, we wished we could find another kind of professor: one to whom the living thing was superior to the pickled cadaver, to whom life bore some relation to living; one who saw a living object as the four-dimensional product of a two-billion-year experience, an object that had a direct bearing on human existence and was directly affected by sharing a planet with us. We couldn't have expressed it in that way, and we needed someone who could. We were looking for someone who today would be called an ecologist.

Donald J. Zinn is that kind of scientist. An internationally known zoologist and former chairman of the Department of Zoology at the University of Rhode Island, to which he came as instructor in 1946, Don Zinn has known for years that there is much to life and living that no scientist can measure or understand. He finds fascination in the unknown, and satisfaction in putting the known into context in the web that consists of human being, animal, plant, and environment. Like many of the earlier biophilosophers, he communicates to his audience that other living things are at least as interesting as people, and occasionally of far more significance to the planet as a whole. It is this conviction that made him a tireless participant in conservation efforts, long before they became fashionable, climaxing his service with three terms as president of the National Wildlife Federation. A lesser, but for his friends and readers almost equally rewarding passion, has been his lifelong pursuit of delicious ways to cook and eat some of the creatures he studies. He is known as a "bio-gourmet" of considerable imagination, and he shares much of his culinary knowledge in this book.

If you are one of those who is aware of the pleasures of beachcombing, of gathering your own mess of clams to steam in a bucket, of climbing a hill for the wind and the view, of collecting leaves for pressing, or fishing without caring what or even if success results, if you believe that knowledge and understanding are worthwhile ends in themselves, you will surely enjoy this book.

—Alfred L. Hawkes
Executive Director,
Audubon Society of Rhode Island

Foreword to the Second Edition

Americans prefer a water-oriented style of life. More than three-fourths of our citizens live and recreate along our coastlines and major river systems. Not only are the coasts and estuaries the greatest magnet for drawing people but, biologically speaking, they are the most productive and valuable of our ecosystems.

The coast provisioned the first American colonists, and provided the sustenance to carry them through the early tough winters and hard times. Those survival experiences of our pioneers proved that human survival depends upon our knowledge and ability to perpetuate the healthy and viable productiveness of land and water upon which all life depends.

The coast, being one of the most important life-sustaining areas, is beginning to falter under the demands of the population explosion. Ever-expanding highways, increasing numbers of homes, and industrialization, often referred to as "New Jerseyization," are taking their toll. The inestimable value of plants and animals along our coast are being adversely affected by the ocean dumping of sewage sludge, offshore oil drilling, untreated toxic effluents, as well as residues from pesticides, insecticides, and fertilizers. Modern technology can help to overcome most of these adverse influences, but only the demands of an informed, knowledgeable, and interested citizenry can bring about change.

Dr. Donald J. Zinn is one of the most respected and knowledgeable authorities on the plants and animals of the coast. This publication is an updated revision of his extremely popular previous work, and contains easily understood descriptions of the plants and animals you are likely to encounter while strolling on the beach. Descriptions and illustrations will be of great help in identifying what you see. The text will help and encourage you in searching for the animals and plants you may not observe at first glance.

The condensed life histories will give you a better understanding of the life-support requirements of the individual species, and the interrelationships of these living organisms with their environment.

The coast is the quintessence of restlessness, and its ceaseless rhythms are forever moving and changing its shape. The sea can be calm and placid at one moment, angry and destructive in the next. Beaches can be enlarged during one season, and diminished or eliminated in the next. Ocean currents can vary in location and intensity, contributing to an ever-changing coastline. This handbook will be of great help in bringing you knowledge and understanding of the coast and its creature inhabitants, and even greater personal pleasure in it.

—Thomas L. Kimball
Executive Vice-President,
National Wildlife Federation,
1952–1981

Introduction to the Second Edition

Strolling along the shoreline at low tide, both the purposeful collector and the casual visitor to the North and Mid-Atlantic Coasts pause every so often to admire for their beauty, their complexity, or their amazing variety the marine organisms and their remains as well as the unexpected and often unclassifiable flotsam that lies scattered about, some partly buried in shifting sand, and some scattered at the bases of cliffs and rocky outcrops. As he continues his wandering, stopping now and then to pick up a choice specimen for his collection or for the table, the curiosity of the beach stroller rises, and he feels the need mounting to find out something about these often fascinating items, to put a name to them and to thoroughly enjoy both the learning and the naming. This is the first reason that this book was written.

The second reason is that the *Handbook* is intended to stimulate the interest of the nonprofessional student of natural science, and the interested layman in the ecologically interesting and environmentally vital coastal shores so significant to many of the socioeconomic problems of the burgeoning population of human shore dwellers. It soon becomes evident to the observant and to the experienced beach stroller that both the sandy beach and the barrier-island shoreline form a dynamic, constantly changing environment that often does not interact well with human trappings. Our stroller must surely reflect that the time has come when humanity must learn to live in harmony with nature at the shoreline, and to understand fully the consequences of doing otherwise. Roger Tory Peterson, internationally respected naturalist, writes, "Inevitably the beachcombing naturalist becomes a monitor of the marine environment."

The emphasis in the second edition is certainly the same as in the first: although updating facts and correcting errors were necessary tasks, much attention was given to improving the coverage of the book and the presentation of the subject. The literature in this field continues to grow at a nearly suffocating rate; transferring such material into a guidebook within reasonable limits of size and cost becomes very difficult.

This volume, then, is still not a complete text, and it is surely not encyclopedic. I present in relatively simple form descriptions and habitats of animals and plants that are frequently encountered in many environments of the North and Mid-Atlantic seashores of the United States. The ancillary material is useful and informative, and, I hope, enjoyable (some of it will appeal particularly to those gourmets with good taste).

In compiling the book, I have utilized every source of information reasonably within my reach, and am consequently under obligation to many people and their publications. Because it is next to impossible to bring such a regional treatise even close to completeness, relevant material has had to be left out. The choices were made by both the editor and the author. I will, however, take full blame for errors and inconsistencies in the text, and will greatly appreciate their being brought to my attention.

I would like to record my great indebtedness to Professor Emeritus of Zoology John S. Rankin, Jr., and to Mrs. Rankin of the University of Connecticut, and to Mr. John Valois, Director of the Department of Natural Resources of the Marine Biological Laboratory in Woods Hole, Massachusetts, for their suggestions and critical comments, and for furnishing specimens on occasion. Mrs. Luella Thompson performed the difficult task of typing the manuscript.

I would like to make special and grateful acknowledgment to my wife, Eleanor, for her valuable assistance and cooperation during the writing of both editions.

Using This Handbook

*T*his handbook is intended to serve as an informal, introductory guide for both the beginning and the experienced lay beach stroller in identifying the commoner organisms found along the intertidal Atlantic shore from Maine to North Carolina, and to suggest the complex relationships between this biota and its environment. To help you study living organisms occupying their unique habitats, the *Handbook* has illustrations and brief discussions of the most prevalent shallow-water species that are likely to be found by the average beach stroller. Most of these are plants and animals that live above or below the edge of the tide, from the high-tide line to snorkeling depths. In this general field manual introducing you to shoreline organisms and their remains, the numerous minute forms native to this environment, requiring microscopes for identification, have been omitted.

It is fair to indicate that probably not all of the animals listed will be seen or collected, and that others not mentioned will occasionally be discovered. This is because the ordinary, constant coastal environmental change brought about by variations in the flow and eddies of the Gulf Stream, meteorological disturbances, fluctuations in temperature, salinity, bottom conditions, and population unpredictably expand or contract the range of some species. It is impractical to allow for all these variables; admittedly, then, the list of organisms in this guide is incomplete.

This handbook is organized on two levels: The first provides a phylogenetic and taxonomic base for the biota, and the second emphasizes broad, easily recognized habitats emphasizing ecological relationships in the shore environment.

The term phylum is applied to each of the main divisions of the plant and animal kingdoms. These phyla rest on radically different plans of structure, and may contain from a few to thousands of species. As might be suspected, there are closer alliances between some phyla than others. Each phylum is divided into subgroups (class, order, family, etc.), to indicate both the systematic position and the relationships of the different species it contains.

In this handbook the phyla are treated in an ascending order of complexity, starting with the so-called simple groups, and proceeding to what are considered to be the larger, better organized, and more advanced taxa. Utilizing a phylogenetic approach also has the advantage of developing a basis for understanding common characteristics, adaptations, and variations within groups, in order to help give a sense of the evolution of these organisms.

Using this manual is a straightforward and easy exercise in observation. When you find and examine a living organism or one of its parts, compare it with the illustrations until you see a satisfactory match. If you manage to recognize only a general similarity or make a probable identification, at least you've found the group to which it belongs. The next step is to consult one of the reference books listed in the bibliography, such as Gosner, Abbott, or Smith to find the name of the species. Then, read the accounts of representative animals in the phylum to which the species you have just collected and identified belongs. A quick reading will help you understand and familiarize you with the group. Many organisms that you will find can be directly identified from a description or illustration in this handbook.

Do not look for an exact resemblance of your specimen to its picture in this book or any other. All individuals, even those belonging to the same species (*Homo sapiens* is a good example), vary in structure, color, form, and appearance from one another. The great nineteenth-century naturalist Louis Agassiz instructed his students of taxonomy to "Study nature, not books." No two animals resemble each other precisely, and nature holds no such oddity as a "typical" individual of any species. A glossary has been provided to help you understand the technical vocabulary that can't be avoided in identification and in my preceding discussion of the organism's environment.

Keep in mind, as the beginning naturalist must, that identification and nomenclature (naming your find) are only the initial steps in learning about organisms, never ends in themselves. Be satisfied with your new knowledge only after observing and studying the living forms in the habitats where you found them.

If in spite of all your efforts you cannot identify a specimen, seek professional assistance at the museum of zoology (or botany) of your state or local university. Specialists at universities and curators at museums are usually willing to help, particularly if your request involves a modest number of species, and if you are considerate of the scientist's other commitments.

Your copy of this manual will be more profitable and will give you deep personal satisfaction if you use the margins for notes—particularly when your own observations of living organisms add to the information already in this text. Take it along on all of your beach strollings.

Selected Beach Fauna—A Checklist

*T*his is a checklist of some of the animals described in this book, with popular and/or scientific names. Each animal is listed in its proper phylum. Although there is occasional disagreement among even the most knowledgeable scientists about the exact ranking, especially when new evidence is presented with the discovery of new fossils or new living animals, each successive phylum is generally considered to be more complex biologically than the preceding group, and so it is presumably more highly evolved.

1. PORIFERA—Sponges
2. COELENTERATA—Corals, Jellyfish, Anemones, Hydroids
3. CTENOPHORA—Comb Jellies
4. PLATYHELMINTHES—Flatworms
   Leptoplana
   Stylochus
   Bdelloura candida
5. RHYNCHOCOELA or NEMERTINEA— Ribbon Worms
6. SIPUNCULIDA—Peanut Worms
7. HEMICHORDATA—Acorn Worms
8. BRYOZOA or ECTOPROCTA—"Moss Animals" Sea Lace
9. ANNELIDA—Segmented Worms
   Sea Worm or Clam Worm—*Nereis virens*
   Plumed Worm—*Diopatra cuprea*
   Gold Tooth Worm—*Pectinaria gouldi*
10. ARTHROPODA—Crustaceans, Insects, Spiders, Millipedes, Centipedes, etc.
    Crustacea
    Common Rock or Acorn Barnacle—*Balanus balanoides*
    Blue Crab—*Callinectes sapidus*
    Hermit Crab—*Pagurus pollicaris*

Lady Crab—*Ovalipes ocellatus*
Green Crab—*Carcinides maenas*
Mud Crab—*Panopeus herbstii*
Rock Crab—*Cancer irroratus*
Jonah Crab—*Cancer borealis*
Spider Crab—*Libinia emarginata*
Pea or Oyster Crab—*Pinnotheres maculatus*
Fiddler Crab—*Uca pugnax*
Mole Crab or Sand Bug—*Hippa talpoida*
Lobster—*Homarus americanus*
Sand Shrimp—*Crangon septemspinosus*
Common Prawn—*Palaemonetes vulgaris*
Sand Hopper—*Orchestia*
CHELICERATA
Merostomata
Horseshoe Crab—*Limulus polyphemus*
11. ECHINODERMATA—"Spine-Skins"
Sand Dollar—*Echinarachnius parma*
Sea Cucumber—*Thyone briareus*
Sea Urchin—*Arbacia punctulata*
Starfish—*Asterias vulgaris*
12. MOLLUSCA—Mollusks (snails, bivalves, squid, etc.)
Polyplacophora
Chiton—*Chaetopleura apiculata*
Pelecypoda—Bivalve Mollusks
Jingle Shell—*Anomia aculeata*
Mussel—*Mytilus edulis*
Oyster—*Crassostrea virginica*
Razor Clam—*Ensis directus*
Shipworm—*Teredo navalis*
Surf Clam—*Spisula solidissima*
Quahog or Hard-Shell Clam—*Mercenaria mercenaria*
Gastropoda—Snails
Eastern Mud Snail—*Ilyanassa obsoleta*
Periwinkle—*Littorina littorea*
Plumed Sea Slug—*Aeolidia papillosa*
Whelk or Conch—*Busycon carica*
Cephalopoda—"Head-Footed" Mollusks
Squid—*Ommastrephes illecebrosa*

Beach Strolling

At nearly any time of year, the sandy Atlantic shores lining our coast from Maine to Cape Hatteras can awaken our pleasurable anticipation of discovering "treasures" of many origins, shapes, and compositions.

Most of the sands on these seashores were brought by currents and tides from the continental shelf and deposited on the beach by waves; some came from weathering of rocks along the coastal regions by wind, waves, and rain, and the rest were transported by rivers and estuaries at their mouths and then deposited along the shore by prevailing coastal currents. A large part of this sand had a glacial origin, being deposited as glaciers melted and formed outwash plains (the broad flood plains of glacial meltwater streams, often underlain by sand and gravel). Every storm, and indeed every tide, every wave, sifts and re-sorts the sand, making it relatively easy for us to see, if we know what to look for, how the beach is continually reworked and remade. The constant motion grinds the sediments, making the sand particles smaller, and scattering them according to their new mass, transporting the small, lighter particles farther than the larger, heavier particles. Thus the higher parts of the beach ordinarily have a deeper layer of fine sand than the stretch along the water line.

Beach sands along this coast consist mainly of crushed quartz of various colors, interspersed with minerals such as biotite, semiprecious gems like garnets, as well as particles of the shells of snails and bivalves. A random sample of beach sand spread under the low power of a compound microscope reveals a granular landscape of varying and sometimes brilliant color and unique angular and rounded shapes, together with bits and pieces of detritus from many sources.

For those who like to collect varicolored and multishaped pebbles and cobbles, there are both exposed beds and secluded pockets of often beautifully smoothed cabochons (egg-shaped chunks) of quartz, feldspars, granites, gneisses, sandstones, phyllites, graphites, argillites, sericites, and conglomerates. Occasionally, a piece of coal or brick, now well rounded, can be found. A fortunate collector may even find one of the small, beautifully rounded greenish "moonstones." "Sea glass," frosted, odd-shaped bits of glass worn by the sea into translucent red, brown, blue, purple, green, and yellow mock gemstones, is also there for the observant beachcomber.

Often the materials most commonly encountered are rows of live, dying, or dead seaweeds along the upper part of the beach, each row left behind at the level of high water. A single line of seaweed represents the last spring or highest tide; the lower of several rows indicates both the height of the last high tide and the difference in height of the two tides. The rows of seaweed are usually composed of species found immediately offshore, although occasionally flora may be mixed in that have been floating and drifting offshore for a long time, such as sargassum (gulfweed). Kinds of seaweeds ordinarily deposited in tide rows along Atlantic beaches, along with the unique marine seed plant, Eelgrass, are the algae: Irish Moss, Palmated Kelp, Laminaria, Rockweed, Bladder Wrack, Sea Lettuce, Sponge Seaweed, Devil's Apron, and Dulse. Adding to our fascinating hunt, all manner of living and dead organisms, as well as inanimate materials, may be wrapped in the seaweeds as they are rolled up the slope of the beach in tidal waters. Here as elsewhere along the shore, the tides and surf leave an occasional packing crate or pallet; a colorful plastic oil drum or pail; an old rubber boot or glove; an orange rind or a poptop; lobster pot or fishing-net floats; pieces of boats, mostly small; and other rich prizes.

Insects are uncommon in all marine habitats. In the tide rows of seaweed, though, live several kinds of biting flies, among which are the greenhead flies; the eelgrass flies; the true seaweed flies whose larvae have been recorded as preying on the eggs of a marine fish; and the chersodromid flies that run about because of their tiny wings. If we kick or otherwise disturb the rotting seaweed, a large number of small jumping animals pop out. These are crustaceans called sand fleas, sand hoppers, or beach hoppers, which feed on the seaweed and burrow in the sand.

On some beaches there may be an abundance of thin, sand-colored collars, two or three inches high. These are the egg masses of the Moon Snail; the eggs are embedded in jelly in the sand collars. Other odd-looking structures are the empty black, rectangular cases with a curled or horn-shaped extension at each corner. These are the egg purses or egg cases of the common skate that have become detached from their subtidal anchorage and washed onto the beach. Very striking too are the spirally coiled strings of parchmentlike discs, about two feet long, each disc containing wedge-shaped compartments with many eggs. These clusters of discs are the egg cases of the large whelks or gastropods; if we pick them up and gently shake them, the shells of the young, probably dead whelks rattle interestingly.

Sometimes the perfect shells of molted crabs, cast during growth, are carried onto the beach by the tide. It is often easy to identify the kind and sex of the crab from which undamaged shells come. Of course, parts of dead crabs and other invertebrate animals are often scattered about, death having come from any of countless natural causes. Driftwood logs, old crates, and other wood debris are common on the beach. Careful searching along the outside of this wood may reveal acorn or ivory barnacles, periwinkles or other snails, and sometimes bits of kelp with strands of lacelike hydroids growing on it, or encrusted with the rounded, perhaps striking colored colonies of ectroprocts or moss animals. The driftwood may also contain the calcium carbonate-lined burrows of bivalve shipworms, or the smaller-bored termitelike tubes of the burrowing crustaceans known as gribbles. It is said that no matter how riddled with shipworms a piece of driftwood may be, its galleries never join or interfere with each other. On some wood, there may even be the twisting calcified white tubes that at one time housed polychaete annelids, relatives of the common sand-dwelling Clam Worm.

All sizes of casts (molts) of horseshoe crab skeletons may turn up on occasion. These casts are often in such good condition, in lifelike positions, that a neophyte must examine them closely to find out whether they are alive. Probably the largest amount of recognizable organic inanimate material along the beach derives from the shells of pelecypods (bivalves) and gastropods (snails). Mollusk shells are found in all stages of fracture and decay: color may be bleached by the sun, chips and breakage are common, edges may be dulled by rolling in the surf and by abrasion. Often, positive identification is difficult. Usually we will do our best collecting in number of species directly after an onshore storm.

Other items that we may occasionally find are various sponges, including the fairly common, light brown, digitate Deadman's Fingers, also referred to as the Eyed Finger Sponge; the floating and attached zooids (including their strings of stinging cells) of the coelenterate siphonophore, the Portuguese Man-of-War (usually in late August); the skeleton of the common Northern Stony Coral, which forms masses rarely larger than one's fist; large jellyfish such as the ubiquitous Moon Jelly, the giant reddish Arctic Jellyfish, the Frilled Jellyfish, and sometimes the Stalked Jellyfish. The tests or shells of such echinoderms (spiny-skinned animals) as the round, dome-shaped pentamerous Sea Urchin are also found; and the thickly gelatinous, massive, compound, translucent gray, tough Sea Squirt (protochordate), which because it suggests salt pork in color and consistency, is known as Sea Pork. Often someone encountering Sea Pork for the first time is sure that riches are suddenly at hand because this common organism looks like a supply of ambergris. Another protochordate (tunicata, phylum Chordata) that sometimes washes ashore in the northern part of the range we are considering is the stalked Sea Squirt or Sea Potato, *Pyura ovifera*. With its long, orange-brown stalk connecting a branching holdfast to the leathery, reddish-brown bulbous body, it looks more vegetable than animal.

Along muddy or mud-sand shores there will probably be elongated heaps of Eelgrass washed up from submerged subtidal meadows of this unusual flowering plant; its long, narrow leaves and the ground around them are often primarily strewn with shells of the Common Northern Lacuna, Halicina Margarite, Eastern Mud and Common Eastern Nassas, bay scallops, and various clams and other mollusks. The cast shells of blue crabs, spider crabs, mud crabs, and an occasional lady crab may also be present. Obvious holes in the surface of the substratum, some with nearby castings that look like miniature cannonballs, belong to fiddler crabs.

Whether outcrops were glacially produced or are of human construction, rocky shores furnish much living material for the collector, but ordinarily flotsam in these areas is not nearly as interesting or as plentiful as in other sea-edge environments. The irregular boulders, cobbles, and rocks along the bases of such structures are somewhat difficult under foot and are apparently more easily and more thoroughly scoured by tides and waves.

Local Habitats

A s with other hobbies and avocations, beach strollers learn that increasing accomplishment comes with continually improved practice, and that refinement of collecting depends on ever more finely tuned observation. Rewards from this naturalist hobby develop for the most part from efficient use of an ever-growing wealth of experience.

Knowledge about the incessantly varying areas inhabited by intertidal invertebrates is of primary importance, and is an accomplishment best gained by personal experience. You win this experience with head and eyes down while you walk along beaches, climb over outcrops of boulders and carpets of cobbles, crawl along groins and jetties, walk among tidal pilings, examine rocky headlands and their tide pools and plough along the edges of salt marshes and estuaries. It soon becomes clear that your best collecting is done on the very lowest tides, when many species (some otherwise unreachable) can be gathered alive, in normally submerged places where shells and tests (hard exoskeletons of nonmolluscan invertebrates) are least bleached and less worn, and where from time to time and with luck, kinds not previously recorded for that area may be found. Do your collecting below the boundaries of low spring tides (at new and full moon) with caution and realizing that in some areas topography and substratum may require special, sometimes elaborate, and often relatively heavy equipment.

To predict the best times for collecting at low tide, consult one or more of these: (1) local newspapers for tidal listings, (2) local tide tables distributed by bait shops and other shore-related businesses, (3) U.S. Department of Commerce Tide Tables (annual), Tidal Current Tables for the East Coast, and (4) the *Eldredge Tide and Pilot Book*, 1985.

Many species are seasonal, and others, because of their biology, disappear at some times of the year but are abundant at others. To make a complete collection from one location, you will do best by sampling at selected stations (sampling locations) at all times of the year. Ideally, such a program should be followed for a two- or three-year period. Professional field naturalists recommend intertidal visits following periods of strong onshore winds, for bad weather, especially gales and storms, can mean successful collecting or an empty pail. An added factor is the position of the tide at the time of the meteorological disturbance. On some exposed beaches, just the constant ebb and flow of the tide, the characteristics of the longshore currents, and the energy of the groundswell waves are responsible for unusual, different, or even reoriented familiar species' turning up daily. These three factors, as well as cyclic changes in water temperatures, cause change in distributions of animals at different times.

Latitudinal Variation

The coastal area from Maine to Cape Hatteras divides biogeographically into northern and southern sections, separated by Cape Cod. From the Arctic to the Equator, ecologists have roughly defined latitudinal marine inshore zones or subprovinces, using their respective mean annual, maximum summer, and minimum winter seawater temperatures. Further, each subprovince has its own characteristic fauna and flora, but these overlap into its neighboring northern and southern subprovinces because of constantly changing meteorologic and hydrographic conditions both lasting and short-lived, and because of the free-living developmental stages of many of the organisms. In this book we consider the Acadian and Virginian subprovinces.

In summer, the water north of Cape Cod (including Cape Cod Bay) belongs to the Acadian subprovince and is always much cooler than water to the south, but the shores of Cape Cod Bay form the northernmost edge of the Virginia subprovince, which extends south to Cape Hatteras. Cape Cod shores harbor fauna belonging to both subprovinces. The Acadian subprovince stretches past Maine and north to Newfoundland. Both of these subprovinces are in turn part of the Boreal province, which reaches along the North American Atlantic Coast from south of the Arctic Sea to Cape Hatteras. The relatively rich diversity of marine fauna and flora along the shores of Cape Cod, it is believed, brought about the unusually productive environment created by the partial bridging of the two subprovinces.

Biogeographical boundaries in the sea act as filters, which explains why the Virginian subprovince has few endemic species (plants and animals native or confined to a particular region), and is transitional, having both southern and boreal forms (species). A good example is the Blue Crab, which passes through both the Cape Hatteras and the Cape Cod filters. The effect of such barriers on the distribution of organisms varies seasonally, with temperature as the main controlling influence. Similarly, we must also consider that water temperature decreases with depth. Many northern cold-water species such as the Lobster, the Jonah Crab, and the Green Sea Urchin are found northward in progressively deeper water, it is thought, because of this decline in temperature.

Intertidal Zonation

"Low water" and "high water" refer to the final levels of the fall and rise of the water at ebb and flood tides respectively; obviously, then, our main interests in collecting and observation as beach strollers are intertidal. Along this coast, every day has two more or less equal tidal cycles, today's tides coming nearly an hour later than those of yesterday. Spring tides have the greatest range between high and low and are best for collectors, and neap tides, occurring halfway through the lunar cycle, have the least intertidal spread. Although the tides are controlled by the pull of the sun and the moon, their range may often be altered by local and offshore weather, especially in shallow bays and sounds. Theoretically, an ideal time to collect would be on a low spring tide with an offshore wind. In the area we are thinking about, the tidal range varies from about 45 feet (spring tide) in the Bay of Fundy in Maine; decreases to about 9 feet along the coast of Cape Cod, and diminishes still further to an average of 3 to 4 feet from Cape Cod to Cape Hatteras. In estuaries, large bottle-shaped lagoons, sounds, and bays, the tidal range varies with the size and shape of the body of water, and often with the wind.

The vertical distribution above sea level of all animals and plants of the littoral (the shore area within reach of water from the ocean; same as intertidal when referring to quiet water without splash or spray) is limited mostly by availability of the substrata on which they live and secondarily by exposure time, desiccation, and extreme temperatures. On the other hand, the lower limit of many intertidal forms is usually set by competition for food, by space, and by predation. The patterns of intertidal zonation that are most distinct most often result from competitive interactions between species.

Rocky Shores

Bedrock outcrops, boulder-laden cliffs, groins, breakwaters, and jetties often give us visible examples of vertical intertidal zones. Ecologists sometimes call this zone the Balanoid–Thallophyte Biome. A biome is a worldwide complex of communities characterized by the prevailing conditions of climate and soil, because it is marine and benthic (at the bottom), and because its dominant members need a hard substratum for attachment. The name of the biome derives from the balanoid barnacles and thallophyte (brown algae) seaweeds that characterize several of the horizontal colored bands typifying this habitat. It is developed best on the rocky coasts of New England north of Boston, Massachusetts.

The strata that form the zone are identified by specific communities of organisms, but, because they overlap at the edges, the divisions are not exact in detail. By oversimplifying them, we can see that rocky coasts generally exhibit three distinct zones: a periwinkle zone (high-tide area), a barnacle or mussel zone, and a seaweed zone (low-tide area). The clarifying names are misleadingly simple: these zones have other fauna and flora, some of them microscopic.

Described in more meaningful detail, the uppermost zone, the supralittoral fringe, receives moisture only from wave spray, rain, snow, or from the very highest tides. The organisms here must be able both to live out of water for a relatively long time, and to withstand extreme changes in seasonal temperatures. The surface of this zone is often darkened by a film of microscopic blue-green algae, and the zone supports communities of rock barnacles and the very few marine mollusks that can stand long exposure to air. Prominent among these are the periwinkles, which in most locations are either the most prominent or the only kind of mollusk present.

The Supralittoral Zone passes almost imperceptibly into the next lower stratum, the Upper Midlittoral Zone. Usually a whitish layer, the Supralittoral, is characterized by seaweeds called Knotted Wrack, and Rockweeds, easily recognizable by the small, bulbous, air-filled bladders on their fronds. Among the crustaceans and mollusks on these algae are scuds and black patches of blue mussels, algae-eating limpets and periwinkles, and the carnivorous, barnacle-feeding dog whelks (their secreted purple or red fluid was used by coastal Indians as a dye).

We identify the next lower stratum, the Lower Midlittoral Zone, by Irish Moss and other types of red algae, and sometimes by clumps of the edible or Blue Mussel attached to the rocky substratum by masses of their unique byssal threads terminally cemented to the hard surface by holdfasts. Other invertebrates in this zone live on groins and on riprap.

The lowest zone is the Sublittoral, exposed only at the lowest tides. As you might expect, the fauna and flora of this stratum are richer than in the zones above. Here, many of the animals hang from or grow on the long, flat rubbery fronds of Kelp that hang in thick tresses from the rocks, and wave in the direction in which the water moves. In this large community live, among others, mollusks, branching moss animals (Bryozoa), hydroids, and tube worms.

Our definitions of these zones have to be somewhat arbitrary, but they make the beach zones each to recognize, and they are reference points we can use in describing where organisms live along rocky shores, and thus where they can be found by the beach stroller. When we observe the biological zones in the field, we can see that they are real in spite of overlapping fauna and flora. Any variation in local conditions, such as wave action, drainage rates during ebb tides, and other physical disturbances of the environment may change the vertical ranges of organisms.

Beaches

Exposed Beaches. The extensive sandy beaches along parts of the North and Mid-Atlantic coasts that are exposed to the high energy built up in turbulent wave action in the open ocean are an unstable habitat. One reason is that the sand is always moving: it shifts a great deal from season to season and from year to year, moved by prevailing tides, currents, and weather. A second reason is that the sand is stirred both by the beating of breaking waves and by the subsequent rush of receding water (the swash). The few sizable animals able to live on such a beach must burrow or move with the tides, and further, the beach has no suitable substratum that seaweeds can attach to. Beach strollers, on much the greatest part of this beach, must satisfy our beachcombing urge with the occasionally large variety of flotsam cast ashore by wave action, including the shells of mollusks such as razor clams, the skeletons of fish, and rarely, a whale bone or other cetacean memento. One scholarly opinion (Pilkey et al. 1980) suggests that because most shells on the North Carolina beaches have been radiocarbon dated to 9,000 years ago, and originally came from the sounds and lagoons in back of the beaches, they can actually be called fossils.

Protected Beaches. The beaches protected by barriers and islands, bordering sounds and lining coves, rarely sustain waves two feet high except during storms. Here the shore exposed at low tide is usually rather steep, and in most places is relatively narrow. You may find that these beaches are interesting biologically, and you will probably be able to make a collection almost entirely different from the life you collected on the oceanfront shore. One difference that will be noticeable is that the substratum is not nearly as uniform, for along with areas of coarse and of fine sand, sometimes in easily discernible pockets, other parts of the beach will be mixtures of sand, gravel, and cobblestones. Walking on stony beaches below the high-tide line requires care to avoid slipping on the moist, algae-coated surfaces of the rocks.

Bays. The beaches in most small bays on the northern part of the Atlantic Coast are so well protected that they have little wave action except during storms. Large bays differ mostly in that their entrances are more extensive and more open to high-energy tidal water, as on exposed ocean shores. Where the bays are actually estuaries into which rivers, streams, or brooks enter, usually an abundance of fine silt has drained from the land. The substructure in such bays can range from fine, mostly clean sand, to real mud, to hard-packed clay. In some places, gravel has worked into the substratum, and in others, rocks of varying sizes may be scattered about, often at high-tide levels. Any one of these bays, then, usually has several different but intergrading substrata along its shores. As a beach stroller, this variation means to you that the fauna and flora living in or on each variety of substratum is usually characteristic of that kind of bottom. In turn you will find that these differing substrata produce a greater spectrum of tests, shells, and other organic materials for you to collect.

This diversity of life forms is further enhanced by the characteristic sensitivity of various species to the range in salt content of estuarine water. The salinity of the substratum (and of course of the water above it) throughout a bay is not always like that of the seawater into which the bay empties. Any estuary, because of its very structure, shows a salinity gradient or gradual change in concentration from the very salty sea water at its mouth to the fresh water at its upper end—and with daily (tidal) or seasonal fluctuations all along the way.

A particularly valuable lesson awaits the serious beachcomber working in this environment. After you are really familiar with the sand and mud-flat material you have collected, and you have carefully observed the detailed anatomy of the collection sites and the creatures living there, you will gradually be able to recognize which animals made the various holes, burrows, markings, trails, structures, and fecal castings that decorate the substratum. With this knowledge your efforts are likely to grow more efficient; they will certainly be more enjoyable.

Salt Marshes. Salt marshes are found along the Atlantic Coast bordering the larger bays, in back of many barrier beaches, fronting ocean shores, and at the mouths of estuaries. A salt marsh is a wetland or swamp in which the water is marine (salt) rather than fresh; its unique feature is exposure to the tides. The landscapes of salt marshes vary in geology and topography; they are typically rather flat and usually have tidal creeks, tidal pools, and mud flats. Each of these features, with its own environmental resources and its own animal and plant ecosystems, combines to make a complex and frequently changing environment. In fact, it is a dynamic ecosystem of unique biological, geological, ecological, economic, and sometimes political significance, and is therefore one of our most valuable resources.

The beach stroller finds the salt marsh an interesting physical challenge. Collectables are strewn in windrows near the shore or along the water at the drift line hidden among the clumps of algae, in the salt-marsh grasses that cover many of the flats, and distributed along the banks and bottoms of tidal creeks and streams. Walking over the grasses, whether at the lowest level through the tall cordgrass, or at slightly higher levels through the diverse salt-marsh plant associations, protect your legs from being scratched by covering them with long pants, and wear sneakers or tennis shoes. Prowling the watercourses presents foreseeable difficulties in making way along soft mud bottoms, and here again it is advisable to protect your feet. It is also well to be aware that in places the soft substratum is so deep that a colleague with a shovel may come in handy for extricating an overeager collector. In such areas, the beach stroller should never venture far alone.

Be ready to spot these kinds of organisms in salt marshes: *below low water*—seagrasses and algae, pipefish, sticklebacks, mummychaugs (killifish), blue crabs, eelgrass; *lower mud-sand flats*—horseshoe crabs, steamer clams, quahogs (hard-shell clams), clam worms, and other burrowers; *lower marsh*—rockweeds, tall cordgrass, ribbed mussels, barnacles, mud crabs; *upper marsh*—short cordgrass, glassworts, sea lav-

ender, marsh snails, fiddler crabs; *upper mud-sand flats*—
beach fleas (crustaceans), termites, crickets, earwigs, and
many more.

Dispersal of Animals and Plants

*P*opulations of animals and plants living along all intertidal
coasts are constantly changing. They are just as change-
able on the northwestern Atlantic Coast as along the sea edge
anywhere in the world. Every member of the marine biota has
its own natural geographic area of distribution, mostly controlled by its biology (locomotion, breeding habits, development, and the rest), and by its environment (substratum, tidal
energy, and so forth). On occasion, species may spread beyond
their usual ranges by means of free-swimming larvae, fortui-
tous transportation on flotsam and, rarely, on jetsam, or temporary vagaries and other perturbations of the environment.

Steady onshore winds may cast up on the beach great numbers of pelagic snails like the violet *Janthuria*. Similarly, beach
strollers may be surprised by low mounds of shells from large
populations of bivalves and snails killed by unusually cold currents or by cold winds at low tide. An area of severe pollution
can produce the same effect.

The geographic range of a species may be altered by abrupt
or slow abnormal climatic conditions, which may be seasonal
or may take years to shift. Among such alterations are expansion or contraction in the latitude of the breeding area, as well
as the kind of local environmental change that caused the Bay
Scallop to disappear during the late 1920s and early 1930s. In
these years, conditions were right for development of a virulent
fungus that caused an Eelgrass blight, depriving young bay
scallops of the leafy stems they cling to as they avoid suffocation
in the bottom mud and muck. When the Eelgrass revived two
or three years later, the scallops also appeared and eventually
rebuilt their populations.

Short-range migrations have been seen in the members of the several groups of invertebrates (animals without backbones). The common Starfish moves from shallow to deeper water when the weather turns cold, and some kinds of crabs and shrimp do the same. In spring, several species of corals and nudibranchs move into shallow water and breed. Limpets and periwinkles make vertical migrations at night, apparently looking for unbrowsed clumps of algae. The Scallop, probably the most mobile bivalve, sometimes moves quite rapidly in schools from feeding ground to feeding ground and to areas with fewer predatory schools of fish.

Gulf Stream eddies and favorable currents, sometimes combined with strong winds and spring tides, may take Sargassum Weed and algae torn from the bottom and roll them in great windrows along the beach with all manner of small animals tucked into their folds, and may also strew concentrations of littoral pelagic (open-water) invertebrates along the shore. Longshore currents may be so strong that this biota may be carried quite a distance from one geographic province to another (usually from south to north). Over the years two striking species of large swimming sea slugs called sea hares have been carried irregularly by such currents along the shores of Narragansett Bay, Rhode Island, and Buzzards Bay and Vineyard Sound, in Massachusetts.

You may be surprised, as many beach strollers are, that some of the animals and plants you chance upon in your peregrinations are not native to North America. Since people began traveling to these shores on all manner of craft, and before that on flotsam, some few hardy, adaptable organisms migrated here successfully. Certainly since Leif Ericson, Bartholomew Gosnold, John Smith, and other explorers arrived, human explorers have accidentally introduced some of the organisms that fouled the bottoms of their boats. Of these, a very few immediately occupied unfilled or sparsely inhabited coastal niches (specialized habitats), and succeeded in adapting to these new environments.

Probably the best-known invertebrate immigrant between northern Maine and Maryland is a mollusk, the common or European Periwinkle, thought to have drifted on logs or other flotsam from Europe to Newfoundland at about the time of the

Vikings, and then slowly spread southward. More recently, human efforts purposely brought several kinds of invertebrates to places in the area covered by this manual, trying to establish mariculture. Among these are lobsters, blue crabs, oysters, and particularly the Chesapeake Bay oysters that were brought to Wellfleet, Massachusetts, after an unknown disease apparently wiped out native Cape Cod oysters in the eighteenth century.

Collecting and Preserving Specimens

What is your reason for collecting the organisms (more often, the remains of those organisms) that you find during your wandering? Every beach stroller's reasons seem different. You may be interested in putting together material for craft work; using your treasures for teaching or as a memento of your visit; learning more about the fauna and flora of the seashore; developing interest in a group of artifacts or organisms; or for gaining first-hand experience and background that will help you understand and persuade others that proper coastal zone management is indispensable.

We can categorize the types of shoreline environments we encounter by the type of substratum and the degree of exposure to wave action. Each combination of features produces a distinctive habitat, each of which supports its own communities of organisms. Do not limit your search to any one part of the shore—start with the lowest exposed areas and cover the entire region to above the highest tide lines. Take time looking around and turning over plants and other material to expose normally hidden surfaces. Masses of seaweeds have been known to hide specimens that are usually hard to find.

Learning to collect efficiently, profitably, and enjoyably is much like learning how to ride a horse: you can get a good start by reading, but beyond initial guidance, such knowledge cannot be absorbed from books; the horse must be mounted and ridden. Get out and do some collecting, and profit from mistakes. Over the years, beachcombing can become so insidiously habit forming that R. Tucker Abbott, foremost American malacologist (student of mollusks), describes the consequences: "casual shell collectors ride their hobby harder and harder until they eventually become severely shell-shocked!"

Observation

Many people have told me that although they had visited the shore many times, they had seen nothing of the great wealth of materials at their feet until they had learned to look patiently and carefully. They had seen a great deal, but had observed almost nothing.

Webster defines observing as, "seeing or sensing, especially through directed careful analytic attention," and seeing as "perceiving by the eye." As there is more to listening than hearing, so too there is more to seeing than sight. To derive greatest enjoyment and satisfaction from beachcombing, to learn about the biology of the organisms you are collecting or about the significance of the artifacts you find, and to appreciate the relationships between the intertidal environment and the shoreline ecosystem, you need to keep refining your powers of observation. People do not enter the world with good or bad powers of observation (no gene has been discovered for "observation"); they develop this faculty by constantly working to refine it. Fortunately, anyone with proper determination will find it possible, even easy to accomplish this refinement.

In *The Wildlife Observer's Guidebook*, by Charles E. Root, you will find several useful exercises, adaptable to your own circumstances, for improving your ability to observe. In the basic exercise, called "Kim's Game" because it was used to train young thieves in Rudyard Kipling's novel *Kim*, a few items (five at first) are placed in a cloth-covered box. The objects are secretly arranged in the box, and the covered box is then placed on a table. When the cover is snapped away, students have thirty seconds to look before the cover is replaced. They must then precisely describe the items in the box and their arrangement. The exercise is continued by repeating the procedure but changing the type, number, and placement of the objects, or reducing the exposure time, or both.

Thoreau wrote, "The question is not what you look at, but what you see." On another occasion, he elaborated this statement: "Many an object is not seen, though it falls within the range of our visual ray, because it does not come within the range of our intellectual ray, i.e., we are not looking for it. So, in the largest sense, too often we find only the world we look for."

How (Field equipment)

The collecting tools of very greatest importance are eyes, hands, and feet, and probably in that order. Protect your eyes from glare and reflection, and perhaps improve your vision with reflecting sunglasses; you'll need help in identification and in studying detailed structure—buy a 3X (three power) to 10X good-quality hand lens (with a protective plastic case), which you can wear around your neck with a strong lanyard (a rawhide shoelace works well). Ordinary cotton work gloves (rubberized gloves in winter) will protect your hands from most splinters, sharp shell edges, barnacle cuts, and other inadvertent but easily infected scrapes. Short fingernails help prevent sand-packed fingertips, and the inconvenience of broken nails. Your feet should be in canvas rubber-soled sneakers or tennis shoes in summer, and in rubber knee-length boots in winter. Many beaches are in tourist country; remember that you'll need protection from the trash of a throwaway generation that seems compelled to litter the intertidal beach with broken glass and metal cans, and from potential injury-inflicting flotsam, which often includes boards with protruding rusty nails. Protection from sunburn and from the excessive exposure that sometimes leads to sickness and eventually to skin cancer is easy to get with suitable clothing, and, where necessary, with sun-blocking skin cream.

Beach strollers do not ordinarily collect live specimens, of course. The field equipment I suggest is therefore designed for inanimate items. To carry specimens, equipment, extra clothing, lunch, and other needs, cheap plastic buckets are almost indispensable. For an extended trip, substitute a canvas knapsack for one of the buckets; it's easier to carry and holds a lot. A long and a short pair of forceps (tweezers), a six-inch ruler, and pencil, and a notebook with plain paper and protective cover to be used for making notes and labels; an assortment of light plastic freezer and sandwich bags for specimens; a protected knife, clawhammer, or prybar for removing collectables stuck in pilings or fixed in cracks; and a trowel to help you remove items from sand or cobbles, complete your collecting equipment. If you can get one, an unmounted crab net or large dip net is very useful for carrying large items that you pick up. To prevent rust and corrosion, after every field trip be certain to thoroughly rinse all equipment in fresh water. If you've any doubt about what to carry on a field trip, a good rule is to take only what you really need, which nearly always turns out to be less than you originally estimated. The proof that less gear—as well as less collected material—is better comes at the end of a long day in the field, when it is time to process and take care of the specimens.

Safeguards

Several precautionary measures should eventually become routine. Safety depends on your using common sense and reasonable care while you work in a marine coastal habitat. Few kinds of wildlife in this environment are harmful: terns that may dive-bomb you when their nests are disturbed, the very few kinds of fish that bite, the crabs that pinch, and the jellyfish that sting. Use extreme caution or avoid handling any fish that appears to have well-developed spines. Respect your allergies, and if you undertake a field trip while under the weather, do not overexert or overexpose yourself to the sun. Always put a small, well-protected first-aid kit in with the collecting equipment so that all wounds, no matter how innocuous they look, may be treated promptly. Approach all intertidal rocks as if they are slippery; most are when wet, no matter how safe they look. When you collect during mean low water on sand flats with very wide intertidal zones, keep track of the tide; usually, flooding here is deceptively rapid, and could lose you both specimens and equipment.

Paralytic shellfish poisoning caused by the "red tide" can hurt us if we eat affected shellfish or otherwise ingest the organism that causes it. The agents responsible for this toxin are several species of microscopic phytoplanktonic (microscopic plants suspended in aquatic habitats) dinoflagellates (group name for these plants) belonging to the genus *Gonyaulix*. They produce untold numbers, forming "blooms," most commonly during summer months in coastal temperate and semitropical waters. The ocean waters that hug the coasts may then be discolored for as little as a mile along the beach to a stretch many miles long, and because the typical discoloration is red or pink, the phenomenon has come to be known as the "red tide." Any filter-feeding marine organism, and particularly mollusks, the edible mussel, cherrystone clam, or soft-shelled clam, among others, can act as an agent for the toxin when it is affected by such a bloom. If you observe an unusual number of dead fish or crabs on the beach, suspect the red-tide organism, and confirm your suspicion by looking at the tide water, for these animals too are subject to the problem. Blooms can last from one day to several weeks. No foolproof method is known for totally removing the toxin, and the best policy is to resist the temptation to collect in affected areas, and to adhere strictly to local quarantine regulations.

Conservation

Our coastal environment is suffering greater damage every day. The shores are attacked by pressures relentlessly applied by the ever-growing population of both residents and tourists and by endlessly varying human alterations. Among these encroachments are coastal construction of marinas, harbors, housing and commercial developments, docks, piers, landfills, and still other kinds of environmental alterations that change and too often destroy shore habitats. All these changes exert direct influence, mostly negative, on the lives of the animals and plants of the intertidal and subtidal waters. Sometimes their influence is subtler, like that applied by effluent from sewage-treatment plants, runoff of contaminated rain from land and rivers, and pollution from petroleum refineries, chemical and power plants, pulp mills, roads, and so on. All these pollutants usually alter the environment and reduce the kinds and numbers of organisms that live there. Because this thin ribbon of rocks, sand, mud, and marsh supports more species than any other ecosystem of similar proportions, it is vital that you and all beach strollers understand and appreciate the reasons for disturbing this fragile environment as little as possible as we pursue our hobby.

Reflect, please, on the bleak seashore that will remain if beach strollers (including all who enjoy this publication) go out and turn over rocks, dig up sand and mud flats, and carry away everything on which we can lay our hands. Destruction of habitat and overcollecting unfortunately have brought extinction to an amazingly large number of animals and plants. Many seem not to care that "extinction is forever." The "prizes-for-the-biggest" syndrome that permeates so much of our recreational activity is a direct legacy from the Dark Ages. Greed and carelessness have no place in the pleasures that satisfy the beach stroller, and indeed they will spoil collecting for all.

Good conservation of natural resources, proper environmental practices, acceptable outdoor manners, and behavior befitting those who appreciate the outdoors strongly suggest that we observe these six rules in the field:

1. Don't catch, dig, or pick up more than you really need or want; leave some specimens behind.
2. Avoid collecting in and thus disturbing unusual natural areas; some of the plants and animals inhabiting them may seldom be seen elsewhere.
3. If you must move rocks, seaweed, and flotsam, do it gently to avoid crushing animals under or beside the disturbed material.
4. Always replace rocks, seaweed, and flotsam as they were, being careful of the organisms underneath.
5. For others' safety, and to protect burrowers in the sand, always fill in holes that you have dug to retrieve specimens.
6. Always obey the fish and game laws, and the beach regulations (local, state, and federal), on collecting and scavenging. This legislation should be available at town halls, local libraries, police stations, and conservation departments.

Preserving Specimens

Live Material. Beach strollers usually are not interested in either collecting, curating (taking care of), or preserving live material. On this fairly large subject many books have been written. These brief suggestions are for the few beach strollers who have the curiosity, interest, and space at home for a few living marine organisms.

After collecting the animals or plants with nets, forceps, trowel, or whatever, the next problem is to get the material home in good condition. Using fresh (oxygenated) seawater at the ambient water temperature of the collecting site, and keeping specimens uncrowded are keys to successful transportation of specimens. Usually four specimens of noncolonial animals or a very few fronds of algae are the practical maximum. You can transport these in buckets or in plastic sandwich or refrigerator bags, much as tropical fish are packaged in a pet store. In the field and on the way home, keep the living material cool and well protected from direct sunlight. Remove casualties and predators promptly.

Have your home saltwater aquarium ready and waiting for the arrival of the specimens. Glass or plastic or a combination of the two are best; wood is difficult to manage for long, and metal will rust sooner or later, with frustrating leaks. Proper filtration and aeration are a necessity for marine aquaria, because without them, bacteria become a problem. Maintaining sufficient concentration of salt is important. Additional information on operating saltwater aquaria may be obtained in Stephen Spotte, *Marine Aquarium Keeping* (New York: John Wiley, 1973); Robert P. L. Straughan, *The Salt Water Aquarium in the House* (New York: A. S. Barnes, 1970); and Paul S. Galstoff et al., *Culture Methods for Invertebrate Arrivals* (New York: Dover Publications, 1959).

Preserving living material is not overly difficult, but it is somewhat complicated, for you will need different methods and techniques for the several processes such as narcotization very often used for different groups of animals. Books that will be helpful are: J. W. Knudsen, *Biological Techniques: Collecting, Preserving, and Illustrating Plants and Animals* (New York: Harper and Row, 1966); E. Yale Dawson, *Marine Botany: An Introduction* (New York: Holt, Rinehart and Winston, 1966); R. J. Lincoln and J. Gordon Sheals, *Invertebrate Animals: Collection and Preservation* (London: Cambridge University Press, 1979); K. L. Gosner, *A Field Guide to the Atlantic Seashore* (Boston: Houghton Mifflin, 1979).

Dead Material

Collecting the biological and nonbiological artifacts that intrigue beach strollers is an orderly and easy procedure. We can pick up mollusk shells, tests of echinoderms such as sea urchins and starfish, tests and shells of other groups of animals, as well as artifacts made of wood, twine, plastic, and other materials, some of them with barnacles, bivalves, or other creatures and algae attached, gently brush away clinging debris and sand, and put them in a bucket or net for transportation home. The best collections are made from the best specimens, and it follows that if we are trying for a collection of demonstrable status, then we will choose only perfect (undamaged) material. Of course, it is always a challenge to identify pieces or fragments of organic remains; as you gain in experience, identifying these makes a good method for examining your ability in identification.

Ordinarily, specimens of the more attractive tests and shells need some "beautifying," an operation that requires careful scrubbing in warm, soapy (soft soap or bathroom soap) water. To remove stains, algal growths, and encrustations formed by other animals, though, soak discolored items in bleach for a few hours, and then thoroughly rinse them in fresh water until the blemishes disappear. Applying a little neatsfoot or baby oil with a clean rag or a soft paintbrush also helps remove some of the unwanted material.

Arranging and caring for human artifacts and natural flotsam both in the field and at home in the workshop or elsewhere is too large a subject to discuss fully here because of the innumerable types of materials that can be found, and the many kinds of things you can do with them. It is most rewarding to consult a few of the many books in the handcraft and woodworking sections of your local library; they will set your imagination going.

Arranging the Collection

Collecting can be a mindless activity if it results only in bucketsful and stacks of evil-smelling, dust-collecting refuse or forgotten, uncared for, unarranged, haphazardly labeled (if labeled at all) jars and other containers of desiccated specimens.

Proper storage requires some work on the easily learned finer points of cataloging and labeling, and on designing and constructing suitable storage and display cabinets. Before starting a collection it will be very helpful to make an appointment with a curator of the invertebrate zoology department in a public, private, or university museum to ask for suggestions and help in solving storage and display problems. Easier still but less satisfactory, you can just visit a museum that has material similar to yours, to observe how a collection can be properly arranged and managed.

To make your collection a source of personal pride, to achieve a sense of significant accomplishment, and to increase the collection's usefulness in accurate identification and suitability for trading if you choose to swap with fellow collectors, it must be well organized and efficiently arranged. You will need to record the vital data about each item fully and accurately: name of the object, name of the collecting locality, name(s) of the collector(s), date of the collection, and any environmental information that is pertinent. Inscribe this information with black waterproof ink on a water-resistant label and then attach the label to the specimen or put it inside the container. Each item will need an acquisition or catalogue number, which you should also mark on the label. Collections are commonly catalogued on 4-by-6-inch white or color-coded index cards, or in a ledger or looseleaf notebook with blank paper and an appropriate number of columns, making the entries with waterproof ink.

Housing the collection simply and inexpensively, and with adequate room for future expansion in egg cartons, small cardboard cartons and boxes, drawers of old bureaus, chests, display cases, hutches, or china cabinets usually is perfectly satisfactory—but to be useful it must be done neatly, and in an orderly arrangement. If you need additional and more detailed information for establishing a credible collection, see R. Tucker Abbott, *Shells of North America* (New York: Golden Press, 1968).

Scientific Names

Species names, the names of kinds of organisms, whether common or scientific, are always a problem for reader and author in a book of this kind. Much of the animals and plants we encounter as strollers along the shore have no vernacular names in common use, so that we must refer to them by scientific name. For very slight reason, nontechnical readers often approach scientific names with suspicion and even fear, or guess that they are an affectation of the learned. Admittedly, common names are easier to pronounce and spell, but the main difficulty is that confusion is inevitable when an organism has different common names in different regions—or a simple term is applied to more than one species. As we all know, another difficulty is the common name, such as snail and clam, which includes a great many species.

On the other hand, scientific names are standardized, and are so well ordered by almost universally accepted rules, that they apply anywhere in the world. In other words, under this system, the same kind of animal or plant has the same name no matter where it is found, who finds it, or which language the finder speaks.

And now for an example. A phylum is a major grouping of organisms (plural: phyla). From the phylum Mollusca (the mollusks), we consider *Mercenaria mercenaria*. This animal is known by many common names, such as Quahog, Chowder Quahog, Little Neck, Cherrystone, Hard Clam, Hard-Shell Clam, clam, or Round Clam, depending on political location and size of the individual animal. In most New Jersey restaurants, a New Englander who wants to order *Mercenaria mercenaria* and specifies Quahogs will see disbelief on the face of the waiter or waitress. In Massachusetts the smallest are called little necks, and the next largest cherrystones, but the names are reversed in Connecticut. In New York, a Conch is a species of *Busycon*, but in Florida it belongs to the genus *Strombus*; a Whelk in England is a *Buccinicum*; here it is a *Busycon*; periwinkles belong to several species of the genus *Littorina*, but it is also a garden flower; and, though *Spisula* is a Skimmer in Connecticut and a clam in New York, a Skimmer is a bird in Massachusetts.

Taxonomists turned to Latin to solve the confusion caused by common names because Latin is an inactive language without a national, popular use; it is uniform, unchanging, and understandable around the world; it is also an analytic language, carrying much of its meaning in prefixes and suffixes, not auxiliary words and word order. Most of the roots used in establishing scientific names are derived from Latin (or from Greek, for most Greek words have Latin equivalents).

Fear of scientific names because they seem difficult (unfamiliar, yes, but difficult, no) is unjustified, and has created unreasonable bias against their use. If we have no trouble with Rhododendron, Geranium, Hippopotamus, or Scorpion, why should *Mercenaria*, *Mytilus*, *Asterias*, or *Homarus* be hard for us? Latin names do not change with usage like English common names, and when they do it is only because systematists have reviewed the classification of an organism in a historic context to determine if a change is necessary.

Scientific names usually consist of two parts: the first refers to the genus (the plural is genera), the second to the species (the plural is species). In *Mya arenaria*, *Mya* is the genus and *arenaria* is the species. If the name has a third part, it refers to a further subdivision; it may be a subgenus, a subspecies, or a variation. The genus, like the surname Jones or Smith, always begins with a capital letter. The species name, though comparable to a first name like Richard, Rhoda, or Robert, begins with a lower-case letter, like roberti. Both parts are always underlined or set in italic or boldface type. The nonitalicized proper noun sometimes found at the end of a scientific name is that of the author who first described the organism, and when a date also appears, it is the year in which the description was published. Thus *Mya arenaria* Linnaeus 1758 means that this species was first described by Linnaeus in an article that appeared in 1758. Invariably, the Latin or latinized names of animals and plants refer to names of people, places, or ideally, to a prominent characteristic of the organism. If you have studied enough Latin to be able to translate names of fauna and flora, you will know before studying the organism one of its outstanding and perhaps identifying characteristics.

A genus may have one species or many. Several species belonging to one genus indicates that those species are closely related to each other. In the general classification scheme of all living organisms, genera belong to families, families belong to orders, orders belong to classes, classes belong to phyla, and the phyla (the main divisions) belong to one of six kingdoms. Where the species of a genus are very numerous and highly diversified, specialists introduce subdivisions. Though necessary, so much analysis often makes the classification overly complicated.

Pronouncing these unfamiliar and formidable-seeming scientific names is seldom more difficult than handling the family names of some of our friends and neighbors. *Webster's Ninth New Collegiate Dictionary* or a good Latin-English dictionary should help with most, and repetition will put the pronunciation into memory for good.

Useful reference works for more information on classification, scientific names, and nomenclature include these: E. C. Jaeger, *A Source-Book of Biological Names and Terms* 3rd ed., (Springfield, Ill.: Charles C. Thomas, 1972); R. E. Blackwelder, *Taxonomy* (New York: Wiley, 1967); C. Jeffrey, *Biological Nomenclature* (London: Edward Arnold, 1973).

Seaweeds

Although most of the vegetation on land consists of seed plants, only two marine species of flowering plants live along this coast: Eelgrass (*Zostera marina*), which grows subtidally on shallow, usually muddy-bottomed bays and sounds from South Carolina to the Arctic, and Widgeon or Witch Grass (*Ruppia maritima*), which is found in brackish bays and alkaline waters from Maine to Texas. Eelgrass is ecologically the more important and certainly more common, and is easy to recognize by its long, narrow, ribbonlike leaves growing from a creeping runner. When older leaves die, they turn black and are washed ashore in great windrows, particularly after strong onshore winds. Eelgrass supports a large population of invertebrates, including the economically important bay scallops. Widgeon Grass is much scarcer, and has narrow needlelike leaves not more than two inches long, growing at regular intervals from a slender stem.

When people mention seaweeds, they nearly always mean algae, the dominant aquatic flora in marine habitats, and specifically the three phyla of the largest of these plants. An alga is any one of a group of chiefly aquatic, internally tubeless plants whose chlorophyll (characteristic green photosynthetic coloring matter) is often masked by a brown or a red pigment. Algae are relatively simple in structure, and usually soft and pliable, with simple, sometimes branching shapes but always lacking roots, stems, or leaves. None of them are woody. Some species have root-shaped holdfasts that enable them to fasten to hard substrata like rocks and shells, and some have small gas-filled marble- or football-shaped structures in the middle or at the ends of branches that give support in the water.

For their structure, reproduction, and especially color, the three phyla of marine algae (seaweeds) are classified as green algae (*Chlorophyta*), brown algae (*Phaeophyta*), and red algae (*Rhodophyta*). Observant beach strollers will easily recognize these groups even after they have been freshly washed up on the beach, and although classifying them in species is often complicated, you can pick out the common forms with no great difficulty if you refer to one of the books listed in the references. Long-exposed dead or dying seaweeds may fade to white or light yellow, or turn green or black, completely different from their original color.

Green seaweeds are found mostly at higher intertidal levels or subtidally in shallow water. The commonest forms are (1) the Hollow Green Weeds (*Enteromorpha*) on rocks, dead shells, wood, mud flats, drifting free, or on other plants, from the Arctic to South Carolina; (2) Sea Lettuce (*Ulva lactuca*) on rocks and muddy bottoms, in brackish pools, and even in polluted areas, from the Gulf of St. Lawrence to South Carolina;

and (3) Green Fleece (*Codium fragile*) on pebbles, and on live and dead shells on the sands below the shallow waters of sounds and bays, from which it may wash ashore in great green, ropy masses and clusters, dragging its mooring. It was introduced from Europe in about 1957, and has now spread from Massachusetts to New Jersey. *Ulva* and *Codium* are edible.

Brown seaweeds are the conspicuous algae of rocky shores in the mid- to lower intertidal zones. The most common species of this group, ranging from New England to North Carolina, are the Black Whip Weed (*Chordaria flagelliformis*); the Sea Potato (*Leathesia difformis*); Ribbon Weeds (*Punctaria* spp.); Sausage Weed (*Scytosiphon lomentaria*), Smooth Cord Weed (*Chorda filum*) New England; Edible Kelp (*Alaria* spp.) New England; Horsetail Kelp (*Laminaria digitata*) New England; Knotted Wrack (*Ascophyllum nodosum*), Rockweeds (*Fucus* spp.) and Gulfweed (*Sargassum* spp.). Of the three species of Gulfweed in the area we are looking at, two are pelagic (free-floating), and one is benthic (growing on the bottom) from Cape Cod to Cape Hatteras on rocks and jetties just below low-tide line. All three are often washed ashore in great numbers because they drift offshore for long periods in huge masses. The 2,500-mile wide area of the Atlantic called the Sargasso Sea harbors Sargassum Weed moving in sporadically occurring windrows in a great circular pattern. These windrows, like miniature coral reefs, are a protective cover in which a unique group of animals shelter, and under which fishes find protection. Ordinarily most of the fascinating and unique community of organisms that live in or attached to the drifting weed, together with the associated flotsam, remain with the masses of Gulfweed when they are beached. Such material is well worth careful examination. We may find, among other things, exotics or nonlocal organisms—strangers from far offshore.

Although greater in variety, the red seaweeds are mostly smaller, less consistent in color, and more delicate than the brown seaweeds. By and large, they prefer warmer waters, need less light than other seaweeds, and are the most common species at lower intertidal levels. The most common forms along the Middle and North Atlantic coasts are: Laver (*Porphyra* species), Newfoundland to Florida, edible; Coral

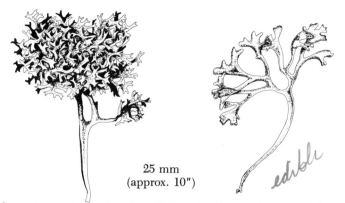

25 mm
(approx. 10")

edible

Chondrus crispus—Irish Moss. The flattened ribless blades expand from a short stock and fork profusely. They are somewhat variable in form and color.

Weed (*Corallina officinalis*), Newfoundland to Long Island Sound; Lacy Red Weed (*Euthora cristata*), Arctic to Cape Cod; Agardh's Red Weed (*Agardhiella tenera*), Maine to Florida; Graceful Red Weed (*Gracilaria foliifera*), central Maine to Florida: Wine Weed (*Ahnfeltia plicata*), Arctic to South Carolina; Irish Moss (*Chondrus crispus*), Labrador to Long Island Sound, edible; Tufted Red Weed (*Gigartina stellata*), Newfoundland to Rhode Island; Dulse (*Rhodymenia palmata*), Arctic to Long Island Sound, edible; Banded Weeds (*Ceramium* spp.), Maine to Florida; Pink Bead (*Griffithsia globulifera*), Cape Cod to Florida; Red Fern (*Ptilota serrata*), Arctic to Cape Cod; Sea Oak (*Phycodrys rubens*), Arctic to Cape Cod; Tubed Weeds (*Polysiphonia* spp.), Maine to Florida; and Chenille Weed (*Dasya pedicillata*), Nova Scotia to Florida.

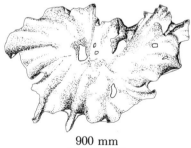

900 mm
(approx. 3')

Ulva Lactuca—Sea Lettuce. Ruffled or lobed unattached somewhat translucent bright green sheets.

The Rich Animal and Plant Life in "The Spaces Between"

Summer occupants of beach cottages and other oceanside accommodations, such as surfers, beachcombers, fishermen, swimmers, sunbathers, and sundry other types of itinerant thalassopsammophiles (beach lovers) who take a little extra time and effort may observe an exciting and little-explored microfauna and microflora living on and between the grains of sand beneath their feet. These microscopic animals and plants live in great variety and in tremendous numbers in the upper layers of Atlantic beaches. We may also find them in large numbers in subtidal sand under water as much as several meters deep.

The easiest way to collect these organisms is to put a small shovelful of sand from about halfway between the tide lines in a large pail with enough sea water to cover it to a depth of about two inches. Take the sample of sand from the surface to a depth of three or four inches. Knead the sand in the pail for two or three minutes by hand, then pour most of the water into a small glass. Examine it there with a strong hand lens. You will see without trouble some of the amazingly active interstitial (the space between particles) fauna and flora. For some of the very smallest forms, you will need a stereo or dissecting microscope.

Another way to collect the interstitial fauna is to dig into the beach at the half-tide line until you reach the water table (at this level the soil is saturated with water). Make the hole big enough that you can swish the water thoroughly with your hands or with a small dip net of the kind used for tropical fish, or a net frame covered at home with the finest marquisette. If you mix the sand and water manually, scoop up the sand water with a small glass jar. If you use a net, invert and dip (wash) it into a similar glass jar containing clear sea water.

The interstitial fauna and flora live in sand and sandy sediments in seas, lakes, rivers, springs, and other bodies of salt, brackish, and fresh waters. We can also find these animals and plants where similar sandy areas border such waters, providing these soils are constantly damp. The biologist's collective name for these organisms is psammon; fresh and brackish water forms are called mesopsammon, and the marine species are known as thalassopsammon.

As a group they are now known as Meiofauna (pronounced May-'o-fóna), or species that live within the interstitial spaces, range in size from 0.05 millimeter (mm) (1 mm = 0.039 inch), and move through the sand substratum without displacing the particles. The thalassopsammon have been studied more often than the others because the interstitial fauna has attained its most varied development in marine sediments. Most of the large categories of invertebrates are represented in the marine sand microfauna, some groups in great variety, and many species display amazingly interesting structure; some represent unique types of organization.

The morphological adaptations (the shapes they have evolved) of both microflora and microfauna to their extraordinary habitat are often little less than fantastic. The animals are obliged to squeeze between the sand grains and glide over the surfaces of adjacent particles of sediment, sometimes on the surface film of water on the particles, and at other times through capillary water among particles. At the same time, they must withstand the rigors of tides, waves, and storms. Natural selection has left most of them with elongated and usually flattened or threadlike bodies, little pigmentation, remarkably well-developed organs of adhesion, various kinds of sensory bristles, and small gonads, especially in the females.

The marine interstitial fauna is a population of often bizarre organisms in an equally unique environment about which only the barest details are yet known. It is a fascinating group biologically, challenging botanist, zoologist, and geologist to discover its origins, relationships, organization, and perhaps even applications useful to the business and survival of humanity and other species.

———————————— *Porifera*

The Sponge—An Ancient
but Efficient Animal

A mong the most primitive organisms along Atlantic shores
is a large group of creatures not fully recognized as animals by all biologists until a little more than a hundred years
ago. The unanswered question was, "Sponges neither move
about nor, apparently, respond rapidly to direct stimuli from
their environment; how then can they capture food?" An imag-
inative investigator thought of suspending tiny particles in the
water near the sponge, and saw these bits of particulate matter
slowly disappear. Further investigation revealed jets of water
issuing from holes at the tops of the animals, and closer inspec-
tion showed that water was constantly entering through microscopic pores penetrating the surface all over the animals. This
discovery eventually led to the now well-substantiated observation that sponges act like animated filters, feeding on the great
variety of microscopic fauna and flora as well as on the fine bits
of detritus (unrecognizable fragments of disintegrating plants
and animals) that ordinarily occur in the waters surrounding
them. This filter-feeding habit also became the basis for the
name given the phylum to which all sponges belong, Porifera,
or pore-bearing animals. Also because of this habit, sponges
cannot live out of water; their whole existence depends on a
continual flow of clean, aerated water passing through their
bodies.

Sponges are thought to have evolved in the Precambrian
period, more than 600 million years ago. They are considered
the most primitive of the many-celled animals: they have neither true tissues nor organs; their cells exhibit much indepen-
dence; all members of the phylum are sessile, or attached to the
substratum; and they display little detectable movement. Although the mists of time make the origin of sponges uncertain,
most zoologists feel that sponges diverged early from the main
line of evolution, and have given rise to no other groups of

9 cm
(approx. 3½")

Microciona prolifera—The Red Sponge. This common sponge encrusts on shallow, hard substrata but develops into large clusters of fingerlike lobes in deeper water.

animals. In other words, they are probably a dead-end phylum.

Sponges are usually found attached to pilings, shells, rocks, and other hard substrata, from the intertidal areas and salt ponds to the depths of bays and sounds.

In some areas, almost every rock bears encrusting sponges on its lower surface, and the submerged parts of pilings, especially those not treated with wood preservative, support many of the smaller sponges. In areas of Narragansett Bay, where oysters still pave parts of the bottom, the dark yellow Boring Sponge has invaded most of their shells, completely dissolving them or making them brittle and useless commercially, and often kill-

Porifera • 47

ing the oysters. The more massive and squatter types, like the so-called Elephant Dung or Fig Sponge, are often found on mud-shell bottoms in the Bay. Still other kinds, such as the Red Sponge, are flat and encrusting when they settle on substrata in shallow and turbulent waters, but are more massive and branching, when they grow in deeper and less disturbed areas. Very often the Dead Man's Finger Sponge, which grows just offshore, is thrown up on ocean beaches.

At last count, sixteen species of sponges were native to the salt waters off the 342-mile coastline of Rhode Island alone. These may be divided into eight genera. *Leucosolenia* are the minute, simply structured, nearly white sponges composed of branching cylindrical tubes that are often found on pilings; *Scypha* are light tan, urn- or vase-shaped, and occur singly or in clusters on pilings; *Cliona* is the brilliant sulfur-yellow Boring Sponge, which is nipple-shaped when removed from its shell substrate. *Haliclona* or Dead Man's Fingers is yellowish tan to gold, encrusting or branched into rounded or flattened fingers rising from a narrow stalk. *Halichondria* or Breadcrumb Sponge is orange-yellow to greenish, encrusting and provided with numerous low, upright tubules, each ending in an opening. *Microciona* is a brilliant red to orange-brown sponge, with fingerlike projections, found both inshore and offshore. *Suberites*, the Elephant Dung Sponge, is yellow to yellowish gray, shaped in low compact mounds and found offshore. *Mycale* varies in color from yellow-ochre to slate gray and often is found on wharf pilings.

Sponges are difficult to recognize as such until we understand their structure and until we positively identify the first one we find. We have trouble because although the large species have generally recognizable shapes, the growth pattern they display is influenced by the type and inclination of the substratum, by availability of space, and by the velocity and type of water currents in which they live. Then too, the dead sponge we find on the beach has lost all its soft parts. It is now a skeleton composed of thousands of uniquely shaped calcareous (calcium carbonate or chalky) or siliceous (glassy) spicules or spongin (horny) fibers, or a combination of these last two found fused together. Beach strollers recognize the sponge by its characteristically shaped skeletal framework, slightly rough to the touch, and often dotted with regularly spaced, small, but obvious openings or oscula. Between the time when the sponge was loosened from its substratum and the time it is washed up on the beach the animals that lived in the cavities and openings of the larger sponges have disappeared. The only evidence that remains of this association is the shell of a mollusk or of a brachiopod embedded in the sponge's skeleton.

Because sponges vary in form from absolute asymmetry (completely irregular) to handsome symmetry, and because they are thought to be so very primitive in structure and function, exactly what constitutes an individual sponge is a question often asked. For sponges with very definite form like *Scypha*, the Vase Sponge, or the large Sheepswool Sponges used for washing boats and cars, the whole sponge is considered an individual. In the low encrusting sponges, though, the answer is more difficult, and here some sponge specialists consider the entire mass as an individual, but other sponge biologists claim that each oscular opening represents an individual, and that the whole mass is a colony. The oscula are round holes large enough to be seen with the unaided eye. Through the oscula, water constantly escapes into the environment after passing through the sponge wall and after being involved within the cellular linings of the sponge walls in both respiration and nutrition.

One characteristic important to both the sponge itself and the biologist are the many interlocking spicules or crystalline rods, made of calcium carbonate or of a silicon compound secreted by special cells, scleroblasts, of the middle mesohyl layer. Spicules compose the delicate scaffolding that is the internal skeleton of the animals. In some species of warm-water commercial sponges off the coast of North Carolina, a tough interwoven fabric of horny material called spongin takes the place of the crystalline spicules, and in other deep-sea Glass Sponges, the silicious spicules join together in one of the most unusual and most architecturally beautiful skeletons in the animal kingdom. The sponge that used to be in every kitchen and bathroom (now we use plastic) was nothing but the skeleton of a Horny Sponge. The infinite variety of sizes, shapes, and combinations of spicules is a vital diagnostic characteristic for zoologists trying to distinguish one species of sponge from another.

Like other animals that are sessile and cannot move around, sponges have larvae that can move. Nearly all marine sponges are hermaphrodites, having eggs and sperm that develop at different times in the same organism. The eggs are fertilized inside the sponge and grow there into minute larvae that eventually go through the osculum into the surrounding water, moving by means of cilia. After a period of planktonic life, they settle and become fixed on a hard substratum, metamorphose, and grow into adults. Many of our local sponges, including *Scypha* and *Leucosolenia*, reproduce equally well by budding. Sometimes the buds separate, but when they do not, the buds make the colony larger and more massive. The regenerative power of sponges is amazing. Some years ago, the zoologist H. V. Wilson squeezed a live Red Sponge, *Microciona*, through a piece of silk into filtered seawater, and within weeks the dissociated cells had come together and formed a complete sponge. Although most of the smaller New England sponges probably live a year or less, some of the larger, deep-water forms may last five or six years.

Sponges, with their calcareous and silicious spicules and their sometimes disagreeable odor and noxious chemicals, make them almost impervious to predation. In the New England area, their only known enemies are sea slugs (nudibranchs) that feed on them. On the other hand, the many structural cavities, especially in the larger forms, provide shelter and sometimes food for many kinds of small crustaceans, worms, echinoderms, and mollusks that, together with their sponge home, compose a unique and interesting community. Some small crabs live commensally (a kind of cooperative arrangement) with sponges, using them for both protection and camouflage. One genus of crab, *Dromia*, cuts and places a small piece of sponge on its back and holds it on with its last pair of legs while it strides about. Gradually the sponge grows over the back, covering it and disguising the crab. Another kind of crab grows *Suberites* on its shell; the *Suberites* eventually dissolve the shell, and the hermit crab occupies a roomy cavity within the sponge. Another kind of association, symbiosis (from which host and guest both benefit) is formed between *Halichondria* and some filamentous green algae. Symbiotic plants are generally important in the excretory processes of the sponge host because they use the wastes of the host in their own metabolism. In turn, the sponge uses the oxygen they release in respiration. Sponges are economically employed only as experimental animals by biologists and in trade between beachcombers and novelty shops.

Similar species, and possibly greater numbers of them, may live on the coasts of the other Atlantic states that we consider in this book, but even the dedicated beach stroller will find very few of them. The reasons are: (1) a great many are so small—they are less than three inches long or broad—or their encrustation or hard substrata are so thin that they are easily fragmented or blown away; and (2) when they die, the soft parts disintegrate and the strong coloration is lost, often making the drab gray or sand-colored skeletons difficult to recognize. Many species vary greatly in size and the usually dull but sometimes brilliant colors of the living animals varies just as much.

Before the secret for manufacturing synthetic sponges was found, the center of the sponge fishery in the United States was Tarpon Springs, Florida, where hundreds of thousands of dollars changed hands yearly in a flourishing sponge trade. *Spongia* and *Hippospongia*, the two genera that had commercial value, were sold for washing both cars and sailboats; they were also adopted by surgeons for use in the operating room. They are still best for these purposes, but a greatly reduced fishery, higher prices, and media advertising have reduced their availability on the market. And yet sponges, the uniquely "simple" animals, are of great interest to embryologists, ecologists, and systematists for extrapolating information in the laboratory and in nature that can be applied to improving human health and welfare.

Coelenterata

Yes, There Are Corals
in North Atlantic Waters

*M*any Southern New Englanders are greatly surprised to learn they have collected a coral skeleton while beachcombing along one of the beaches sloping along the shores of Massachusetts, Rhode Island, and eastern Connecticut; aren't corals found only in warmer southern waters? Of course most of them are reef-forming animals that live mainly in tropical salt waters, as off Southern Asia, Bermuda, and in the Caribbean, where the minimum water temperature is about 70° Fahrenheit (21° Celsius).

A few species of non-reef-forming corals live individually as small colonies in cold waters at moderate depths as far north as the Arctic Ocean. These are the madrepores or stony corals, and it is to this group that *Astrangia astreiformis* (formerly *danae*), the Star Coral, belongs. The only coral in these waters, it lives as far south as Florida.

On stones or shells picked up along the beach, one often finds the encrusted skeletons of star coral colonies. The tiny cuplike depressions or tubular prominences, about an eighth of an inch in diameter, were the sites of the individual coral animals. Five to thirty individuals live in a colony, held together by the calcium carbonate deposited by the organisms.

If the edges of the cups are rounded, the colony has probably been dead for some time, its borders having been worn away by waves that ground it along the bottom and up onto the beach. If the edges are sharp and the details of the skeleton are clear, though, it is a recently dead colony and is more valuable to the collector.

Corals, seafans, seapens, and the closely related sea anemones (found on pilings, boulders, submerged logs, stones, and shells throughout Atlantic bays and salt ponds) belong to a still larger group of animals, the coelenterates, which also includes

.3 cm
(approx. ³/₁₆″)

Astrangia astreiformis—The Star or Northern Coral.

jellyfish, the Portuguese man-of-war, and hydroids. All these
(1) are radially symmetrical, (2) have one opening into the
body, and (3) have complicated stinging cells (nematocysts).

The coelenterates are generally considered to be quite primitive and among the lowest of the many-celled animals. Their
reproductive capacities, though, are peculiarly well developed.
Some species have separate sexes and others have both sexes in
the same individual (hermaphrodites). Sexless or asexual reproduction rules in many other species.

A great many forms are still more complex—their life cycle
is curiously divided into a sexual (medusa, the swimming
stage) and an asexual (polyp, the sessile stage) part. One part
apparently alternates with the other. The star corals are coelenterates that have only the polyp or sessile stage, whose hoved
skeleton we encounter intertidally in the sand.

Living individuals are both beautiful and graceful. The
slightly bluish or pinkish transparent polyps extend about ¼
inch above the opaque calcareous base. The edge of the extended disk bears a circlet of stubby, fingerlike tentacles whose
tips glisten white with light reflecting from large numbers of

Coelenterata • 55

nipple-shaped batteries of the stinging cells. When a minute crustacean or other microscopic organism touches a tentacle, this living food is subdued by the nematocysts and is thrust toward the central rounded mouth by the folding of the stimulated tentacle acting in concert with its neighbors. The prey is quickly engulfed by these carnivorous animals. The transparent body wall of the polyps shows the edges of the internal partitions or mesenteries (septa), whose number, distribution, and size we need for identifying coral species.

When polyps die, the soft body parts quickly decompose and are washed away, leaving only the hard calcareous base or skeleton. In these corals, this structure, almost entirely calcium carbonate, is secreted by and is built up around the base of the body in the form of a cup into which the soft parts can retract. The entire polyp grows upward, the hard part by additions to its base, and it divides or buds, eventually attaining the normal stature of the star coral colony. The hard calcareous base is the so-called stony material that gives these corals their name.

A new colony is started when an egg from one coral individual is fertilized by a sperm from another individual. The embryo grows into a microscopic platterlike ciliated organism that becomes a member of the fantastically numerous legions of minute animals suspended in water (zooplankton) for a short time before settling on suitable substratum and metamorphosing into a coral polyp, progenitor of another colony.

Jellyfish—Made of Water But They Cover the World

*E*ver since sailors conquered the seven seas, waterborne travelers, fishermen, and swimmers have wondered about the many sizes and kinds of jellyfish. These are among the most familiar and common animals in shallow water along the shores and off the islands that dot the North Atlantic coast.

A free-living bell- or umbrella-shaped organism, structured of stiff gelatinous material, the Jellyfish or Medusa either

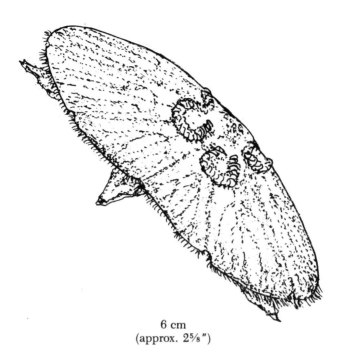

6 cm
(approx. 2⅝")

A side view of *Aurelia aurita*—The White or Moon Jellyfish. The horseshoe-shaped structures are gonads.

swims (convex shape forward) with more or less rhythmic pulsations using a contractile sheet of muscle near the outer rim, or floats in the water at the mercy of wind, wave, or current. The radiating network easily seen through the jelly is made up of canals branching from the stomach carrying food and oxygen-laden sea water.

The bodies of jellyfish combine more than 95 percent water with minerals and organic material to form a strong and often quite resilient jelly.

These animals belong to the most primitive phylum of true metazoans (many-celled animals), the coelenterates, a name describing the central "intestine" as the sole body cavity. Coelenterates also include such animals as anemones, corals, hydroids, seapens, seafans, and the Portuguese man-of-war.

Jellyfish, like other coelenterates, are radially symmetrical: a central axis goes from the upper surface to a mouth sometimes

Coelenterata • 57

surrounded by multiples of four or six variously shaped arms on the base. The parts of the animal are arranged concentrically around this axis.

The tentacles are very noticeable—short and stubby or long and slender extensible projections around the rim at the lower end in one or more whorls. Jellyfish have no head, no centralized nervous system and no definite respiratory, circulatory, and excretory systems.

Many species of coelenterates alternate in a life cycle of two visually distinct morphological types. One type is the polyp, a sessile or sedentary, essentially tubular structure, ordinarily attached at one end to a hard substratum by a basal disk or by projecting rootlike branches; the other end terminates in a circular mouth surrounded by a varying number of tentacles. It reproduces asexually by budding off from special structures (gonangia). The other morphological type, commonly called jellyfish, is the motile Medusa.

The Jellyfish or Medusa is either male or female and ordinarily has four horseshoe-shaped gonads, equidistant in the same plane, bearing eggs or sperm. The sexual products are shed and fall into the water, fertilization takes place, and a microscopic, flat, platter-shaped ciliated larva (planula) is produced. After a usually short planktonic existence, the planula settles to a suitable substratum and changes into a polyp type of individual, completing the life cycle.

Jellyfish eat large or small passing prey by snaring and paralyzing them with the trailing tentacles, which then contract, drawing this food to the mouth. The larger jellyfish are capable of capturing relatively large fishes, ingesting large or small prey whole. Some jellyfish eat other jellyfish; smaller jellyfish feed on plankton and organic particles accidentally entangled in the mucus on the surface of the bell. Microscopic whiplike flagellae carry this material to the edge of the bell, where additional currents transfer it to the mouth along the lower surface of the bell. Sea turtles live somewhat on a diet of the large oceanic jellyfish, but the giant ocean sunfish, *Mola mola*, depends much more on it.

Well over 2,000 years ago, Aristotle, in his epic work in natural history, *Historia Animalium*, had a great deal to say about the coelenterates, particularly about the medusae. Even into the nineteenth century, biologists took their apparent combination of plant and animal characteristics as a reason for classifying them with marine plants. Ellis, Tremblay, Peyssonel, and later the great Louis Agassiz, deciphered the biology of coelenterates. G.O. Mackie, a specialist in coelenterate neurophysiology and neuroanatomy, is satisfied that Agassiz was the first to acceptably describe nerves in a coelenterate. Many coelenterates are found as fossils; both relatively complex corals and jellyfish appear in rocks dating back more than 400 million years.

People have long been actively aware of the coelenterates whose nematocysts are capable of inflicting painful stings. Fortunately, just a few groups of jellyfish have nematocysts capable of penetrating human skin. Along with the hydrozoan siphonophores, the major groups of stinging coelenterates belong to a class of large, specialized jellyfish known as the *Scyphozoa* or Sea Nettle. One particularly dangerous type, the Sea Wasp, is found in the tropical waters of Australia. Less hazardous is *Cyanea capillata*, the so-called Pink Jellyfish, the giant or arctic jellyfish of the Atlantic Ocean (known to Sherlock Holmes) with a lens-shaped disk that may reach a diameter of eight feet, and 800 trailing tentacles that may extend 200 feet into the water. Ordinarily the *Cyanea* south of Cape Cod and in Narragansett Bay are smaller and relatively harmless, rarely larger than a foot in diameter.

The Portuguese man-of-war, sometimes found in the fall, is joined by *Cyanea* (to mid-June), and other large jellyfish in North Atlantic coastal waters, including a number of species of the small hydrozoan and of the microscopic interstitial hydroid medusae; *Gonionemus murbachii*, sometimes in eelgrass; yellow green *Liriope scutigera; Haliclystus auricula* or Stalked Jellyfish, a small, variously colored, curiously attached medusa that lives as if it were an anemone; *Periphylla hyacinthina*, with a high, narrowly pointed bell; *Pelagia cyanella*, purple-rose to blue, luminescent at night; and *Dactylometra quinquecirrha*, the Frilled Jellyfish, with forty golden yellow tentacles. Perhaps the species we see most often washed up on beaches in Southern New England is *Aurelia aurita*, the common and abundant "white sea jelly" or Moon Jelly, with a relatively flattened, saucer-shaped, milky white disk, often contrasting with the prominent pink, horseshoe-shaped gonads of the male.

The stinging cells or nematocysts of jellyfish are distributed widely over the surface, especially about the mouth and the tentacles, where they may be gathered in warlike clusters of nematocyst batteries. The nematocysts are anchored in underlying tissue by a rootlike structure, and the exposed end terminates in a bristlelike trigger. When the trigger is released by mechanical or other stimulus (discharge response is independently controlled by each nematocyst), a coiled tube springs from the flask-shaped cell, discharging the contents of the cell-reservoir into the environment or into the object touched. Once released, a nematocyst cannot be used again.

The "sting" of most jellyfish is not perceptible to man. Of course we, like other species, have a great deal of individual variation and thin-skinned, very young, allergic, and similarly incapacitated people suffer far more than their opposites, Even in the relatively less dangerous northern waters, approach most very large jellyfish with caution: *Cyanea* produces a burning sensation and *Dactylometra* can cause lesions and illness as well. The poisons are alkaloidal and may include such compounds as thalassin, congestin, and hypotoxin. The more serious manifestations of jellyfish contact may result from anaphylactic shock, especially for someone who may have been stung previously by the same species.

In the field, it is well to respect all true jellyfishes; make it a rule to observe them from a safe distance, and then if you must approach them, do so cautiously. It takes a good reason to handle jellyfish at all. At best, they are difficult to preserve; by the time they have washed ashore they are invariably damaged; and in our unnatural and destructive (for them) environment, identification is for experts. Remember that tentacles can retain their stinging power for a long time, and that even dried stinging cells may revive when wetted. A couple of good rules of thumb are: (1) avoid handling large jellyfish on the beach, especially Portuguese men-of-war, sea wasps, and sea nettles, and try to stay clear of them altogether in the water; and (2) take it for granted that contact with any of them will produce stings—it is next to impossible to always recognize on sight the ones that will give trouble.

Treatment for jellyfish stings: Thoroughly wash the affected area of the skin with a harsh soap such as tincture of green soap, then apply calamine, alcohol, vinegar, bluing, witch hazel, bicarbonate of soda paste, or other soothing lotion. For severe cases, apply ice packs and see a physician as quickly as possible.

Anemones for Beach Strollers

Soft-bodied Sea Anemones are rare finds out of water. Essentially they are corals lacking a calcium carbonate skeleton. These columnar or cylindrical coelenterates have an adherent pedal disk at one end, on which they can slowly glide on a hard substratum—usually pilings, rocks, and tide pools; a few species burrow in sand or sand-mud mixtures. The other end of the anemone bears one or more rings of tentacles that surround the mouth and help ingest small live or dead plankters (plankton organisms) and live or dead fish. Anemones can retract their tentacles and shrink their columns to a soft blob when they are disturbed. They vary greatly in color, being of almost all hues, though none are black; and many have blotches, stripes, or streaks in contrasting colors. The species range from as small as one-quarter inch to more than four inches. Anemones are so often difficult to identify that we should have species verified by a university or museum specialist.

Hydroids for Beach Strollers

*H*ydrozoans (or hydroids) are a large class of coelenterates, with about 250 species living between Maine and Cape Hatteras. But because they are mostly small and delicate, we will seldom find them except clinging by their thread-sized, stolonlike stems to exposed rocks, shells, pilings, larger hydroids, and seaweeds, sometimes as single strands and sometimes as large networks.

Two exceptions are the Snail Fur (*Hydractinia echinata*), colonies of which encrust snail shells or hermit crabs with a pinkish or brownish fuzz, and the tubularian hydroids, whose dense six-inch-long pinkish growths on pilings, groins, and other surfaces wash ashore intertidally in tangled knots of whitish, battered stems.

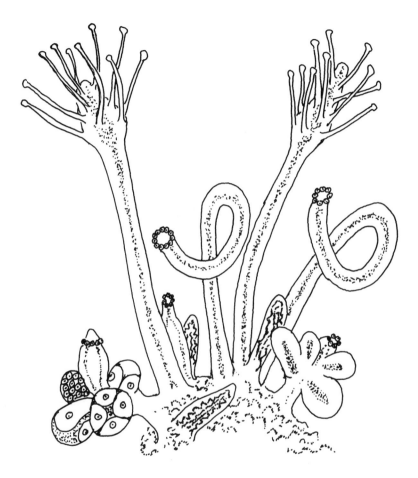

5 mm
(approx. ³/₁₆″)

Hydractinia Echinata—Snail's Fur. Colonies mostly encrust snail shells containing Hermit Crabs. These expanded polyps of various shapes, sizes, and functions emerge from stolons embedded in a brownish crust.

Coelenterata • 63

Ctenophora

The Jellyfish That Isn't

*I*n August and September, if you swim in the coastal waters of Massachusetts, Rhode Island, and Connecticut you are likely to encounter small walnut-shaped, nearly transparent, delicate, jellylike planktonic animals, the so-called comb jellies, sea walnuts, or sea gooseberries. These ctenophores ("comb-bearers") are commonly washed, blown, and driven into windrows and slowly circulating masses against the sides of docks and in the lee of boats at anchor, or against gently sloping subtidal sands. Our natural reaction is to think we are bumping into jellyfish and that we will be painfully reminded of these accidental encounters. Of course we would be wrong on both counts; comb jellies belong to a different phylum from jellyfish, Ctenophora rather than Coelenterata, and with one small exception that is not found in these waters, no comb jellies have stinging cells.

Comb jellies live in all the oceans to depths of more than 10,000 feet, and are often found in unimaginably large numbers. The eight rows of characteristic ciliary combs radiate over the surface of the animal from the upper to the lower pole like the lines of longitude on a globe of the world. The cilia on each comb beat as one, and the eight rows of combs beat synchronously, propelling the animals so slowly and feebly that they are at the mercy of currents and tides. They may swarm in natural or artificial embayments for a few days; then, just as quickly, they disappear, moved by the waters. Very often an ebbing tide will leave large numbers of them as gelatinous blobs along the water's edge, soon to dry and vanish from sight.

In this vicinity, two kinds of ctenophores are common: the one-inch-long *Pleurobrachia pileus*, the Sea Gooseberry, and the larger bilobed *Mnemiopsis leidyi*, the Sea Walnut. The conical, ovate, thimble-shaped *Beröe ovata* (named for a

66 • Ctenophora

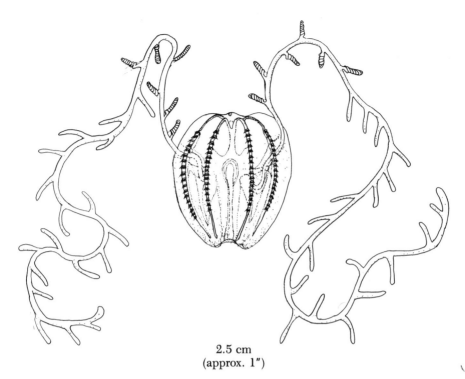

2.5 cm
(approx. 1″)

Pleurobrachia pileus—The Comb Jelly.

daughter of the Greek sea god, Oceanus), which lives in large
swarms and is known for its voracity, sometimes swallowing
small fish and other ctenophores slightly larger than itself, is
abundant from Chesapeake Bay to Florida. *Cestus veneris*, the
Venus Girdle, is a ribbon-shaped, transparently iridescent
ctenophore about three feet long by three inches wide that lives
in tropical seas. Fragments sometimes are washed ashore by
Gulf Stream eddies. On this coast, *Pleurobrachia* is found from
Long Island to Greenland, and *Mnemiopsis* is distributed from
Vineyard Sound to the Carolinas.

The first recognizable account of a ctenophore in the recorded history of biology was in 1671, and for a long time these
animals were grouped indiscriminately with the jellyfish as
Acalephae or "nettles"; later on, they were placed with the
coelenterates. Not until 1889 were they removed from the jellyfish, coral, hydroid phylum and established as a separate
group. Compared with coelenterates, ctenophores are mono-
morphic (only one kind of adult); with one small exception,

Ctenophora • 67

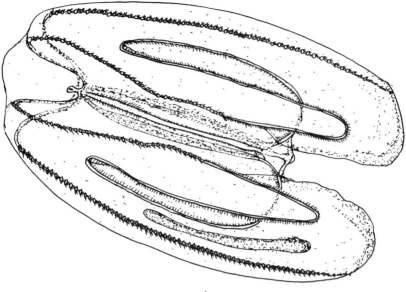

4 cm
(approx. 1⅝")

Mnemiopsis leidyi—The Sea Walnut.

they lack nematocysts (stinging cells); they have significantly more highly developed muscular, digestive, and sensory systems; and they have eight rows of ciliary plates, "combs," throughout life. A unique anatomical structure is the *aboral* (end opposite the mouth) sensory organ. Relatively complicated morphologically, this organ enables the animal to detect changes in orientation. Ctenophores are composed of 93 to 95 percent water (making them difficult to preserve); the solid material is chiefly salt, with less than 1 percent organic material, most of which is protein.

Pleurobrachia has a pair of very long, highly contractile filaments, each with similar short lateral branches. The filaments may be contracted at will into pitlike tentacle branches. The filaments or tentacles are covered with adhesive cells (colloblasts) that hold prey fast while the tentacles retract and draw the adhering food within reach of the mouth.

Rowing, sailing, or motoring through a swarm of ctenophores at night can stir spectacular bioluminescence in the sea. Both bow wave and stern turbulence will be outlined with brilliant flashes of blue-green light that comes from the meridional canals of whole or damaged animals. According to R. Buchsbaum, "The rapidly beating combs refract light, and produce a constant play of changing colors. Comb jellies are noted for the beauty of their daytime iridescence, but this is certainly matched at night by those comb jellies that are luminescent. When the animals are disturbed as they move through the dark water, they flash along the eight rows of combs."

The high percentage of water in their tissues makes ctenophores prone to mechanically caused wounds. Such damage need not be fatal, for these fragile animals have a great capacity for replacing and repairing any part that is damaged, destroyed, or lost. Apparently all members of this group are hermaphrodites (both sexes in the same individual), ovaries and testes being found in meridional canals. Both eggs and sperm are shed into the surrounding sea through the mouth, and fertilization ordinarily takes place at once. It is quite possible and even probable that self-fertilization is the rule rather than the exception. The young are also planktonic, and closely resemble the adult in form and function.

Although several species of ctenophores are commensally associated with such other organisms as gorgonians, soft corals, starfish, and sea urchins, this type of existence has not been observed thus far in our coastal forms. The distribution of the commensal species may be limited by that of their hosts.

On the other hand, the long (1¼ inch), thin, pink actinarian (sea anemone), *Edwardsia leidyi*, can often be seen through the body wall of its host, *Mnemiopsis*. This is an uncommon form of biological association, a coelenterate parasitizing a ctenophore.

All ctenophores are carnivorous, living on crustaceans and other planktonic animals as well as small fishes. A large swarm of ctenophores can easily decimate the other zooplankton living in an area.

Platyhelminthes

Marine Flatworms

*T*he minute, delicate-textured turbellarians that live
among the sand grains of intertidal beaches up and down
our coast are the local representatives of the group of soft-
bodied free-living flatworms that belong to the phylum Platyhelminthes. Their larger relations can be found moving over
Sea Lettuce (*Ulva lactuca*) in the tidal flats, gliding and undulating over stones and shells subtidally, swimming by rhythmic
rippling motions just below the tide zone, or inhabiting empty
shells of hermit crabs and whelks.

Marine flatworms are elongate, narrow, flattened, and more
or less leaf-shaped. They range in length from less than half an
inch (1¼ cm) to two inches (5.0 cm) and are usually drab in
color. These animals are carnivorous, and the mouth, the only
opening in the body, is well back from the anterior (front) end
of the ventral (under) surface of the body. A tubelike proboscis
(the pharynx) is extended from the mouth to the microscopic
organisms—small worms, snail eggs, and others—on which
they may be feeding, and digestive juices are poured onto the
food, which is somewhat liquified before being sucked into the
body. In some species, the extensible pharynx expands like a
thin-walled trumpet before it envelops its prey. Flatworms
glide over the bottom of submerged plants and other materials,
or propel themselves through the water by nearly invisible
waves of muscular contractions, along with coordinated movements of their microscopic hairlike structures (cilia). They are
hermaphrodites possessing both testes and ovaries, but cross-
fertilization of two individuals always takes place. The eggs are
laid in small patches of slender-stalked, dark-brown-to-black
cocoons, usually fastened to the underside of rocks, and the
free-swimming larvae become temporary members of the zooplankton. The smallest forms such as the light brown *leptoplana* are found ordinarily under rocks near the low-tide line,
and the larger and more strikingly colored yellow-banded

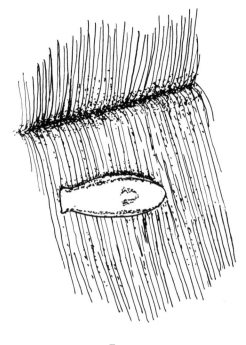

.7 cm
(approx. ⁵/₁₆″)

Bdelloura candida—A light brown flatworm most commonly found inhabiting the gill plates of the hermit crab.

brown *Stylochus* live mostly in dead shells. Flatworms may be found on and under rocks and seaweed or gliding over a variety of surfaces in their never-ending quest for food. The common flatworm on drifting Gulfweed is the brownish, spotted *Gnesioceros sargassicola*, a 9-millimeter-long turbellarian with two small tentacles covered with eyespots, and a cluster of eyespots on the head in front of each tentacle. The inch-long, spearhead-shaped, white-to-brownish-yellow species, *Bdelloura candida*, lives on the gill plates of the Horseshoe Crab.

Behaviorists and biologists use the larger flatworms as experimental animals to study both their remarkable power of regeneration and the relationships between sense organs and movement. The free-living flatworms have aroused a great deal of attention. Ethologists have found from experiments that not only may they be able to store information but that experience may condition their future behavior. When it was discovered that flatworms normally seek dark areas, and, given the oppor-

Platyhelminthes • 73

tunity, will move from light to shade, they were trained by repeated physical restraints to make fewer and fewer attempts to avoid the light. More spectacular experiments showed that this kind of training could be transferred from a trained to an untrained individual by simply feeding the trained worm to the untrained one. Perhaps the climax of this work was reached by investigators at the University of Michigan, who trained flatworms, then cut them in half to find out how much acquired learning each regenerated individual retained. It turned out that the flatworm's tail has as good a memory as the head. A by-product of this and subsequent work was the researchers' publication of *The Worm Runner's Digest*. The publication mixes fact and fun, for as the editor, James V. McConnell of the University of Michigan, says, "it seems to me that anyone who takes himself or his work too seriously is in a perilous state of mental health."

A few of the so-called free-living flatworms are symbiotic: they spend a part of or even their whole life cycle more or less intimately associated with a different or larger species of animal in a functional exchange. In these worms the exchange is moderate; ordinarily one partner does not depend absolutely on the other. Some of the marine forms are internal parasites in the body cavity of a species of a local isopod, *Idotea*, as well as in several kinds of hermit crabs. Other parasitic turbellarians have been found in brittle stars (ophiuroid echinoderms); in pelecypods (bivalves) such as *Teredo* the shipworm, the mussel *Modiolus*, and the cockle *Cardium edule*; and in several species of gastropods (snails). It is quite possible to find a ray in the catches of local seiners and trawlers that bears on its surface the turbellarian, *Micropharynx*. The best known of all symbiotic flatworms, though, may be the predacious so-called oyster leeches that penetrate the shells of the local oysters (*Crassostrea*), and feed on the soft parts.

— Nemertinea, Sipunculida, Hemichordata

Little-Known Vermiform
Denizens of the Tidelands

*E*xplorers of the mixed sand and the sand sediments that cover the bottom along a great deal of the Atlantic Coast shoreline will sooner or later, with careful digging, come upon members of three quite numerous but little-known groups of unsegmented worms: the ribbon worms, the peanut worms, and the acorn worms. Although it is fairly easy to separate the smaller and more colorful acorn worms from the two other groups, and though ribbon worms are slightly flattened and peanut worms are quite rounded, the three kinds of worms belong to three totally different categories or phyla of the animal kingdom and are almost entirely unrelated.

The nemertines (Nemertinea) are commonly known as ribbon worms or proboscis worms. They are a phylum of contractile, soft-bodied, subcylindrical, greatly elongated worms, from two inches to six feet in length. They are unsegmented and thicker and longer than flatworms. Their most unique structure is a thorn-armed proboscis contained in a sheath inside the body that can be shot out rapidly at great length from an opening close to its anterior end. The proboscis can wound and wrap around such living prey as mollusks, crustaceans, and other worms, and draw this prey to its mouth. Most ribbon worms, especially broader types (*Cerebratulus*), burrow in the mud or sand, or live on rocky shores along and beneath the rocks. The narrower forms, such as *Lineus*, dwell in mussel beds; *Tetrastemma* lives on and around seaweeds, or like *Oerstedia* is commonly found on pilings. Some species form semipermanent burrows lined with mucus, and a few live in distinct mucoid tubes of sand. A small yellowish-white wormlike form, *Malacobdella*, is symbiotic, and lives in the mantle cavity of the Steamer Clam, *Mya arenaria*. *Cerebratulus lacteus*, a white, active six-foot worm, swims at night in tidal and

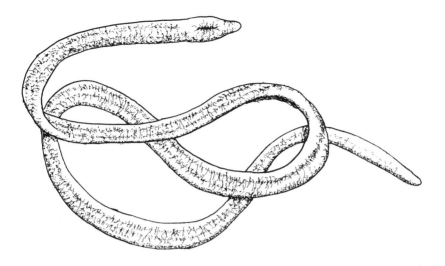

Cerebratulus lacteus—The largest of American shallow-water nemerteans or ribbon worms, sometimes reaching a length of 6 meters.

subtidal water with the typical undulating motion of ribbon worms.

Most nemertines move by gliding over the substratum in a trail of self-produced slime, propelled by surface cilia. Their tendency to break into pieces when disturbed or otherwise irritated can be frustrating to the collector (as it must be to preying crabs). Each of the pieces, however, can grow into a complete animal.

Because of their regeneration, nemertines have been a favorite subject for biologists interested in asexual reproduction. All species of marine nemertines copulate, the sexes are separate and they either produce their young alive, or shed eggs and sperm into the water. All pass through a free-swimming larval stage before settling to the bottom and undergoing complicated metamorphosis into a young worm.

Peanut worms or sipunculids are a relatively small group of worms whose common and only representative in North Atlantic coastal waters is *Phascolosoma gouldi*, the Peanut Worm, often a foot long. According to W. D. Russell-Hunter, *Golfingia*, a close relative of Phascolosoma, received its generic name after being discovered by the well-known zoologists, W. C. McIntosh and E. Ray Lankester, in the muddy shores of the "Royal and Ancient" golf course at St. Andrews, Scotland. Unfortunately, the name *Golfingia* has been changed to *Phascolopsis*.

Peanut worms are drab-colored, sedentary, and abundant in shallow waters. Their active burrowing in mud and sandy mud produces temporary tubes filled with mucous secretion. The unsegmented cylindrical body, through whose smooth walls you can see longitudinal muscles, is continually expanding and contracting, making its shape quite variable. In burrowing, the animal everts its proboscis (introvert) into the sediment, enlarging this end to form a mushroom-shaped anchor, and then pulls the body toward this enlargement by contracting the strong muscles in its body wall. The introvert is an expandable, long, slender organ that can be quickly telescoped into the body when the animal is disturbed. The mouth is at the front of the introvert and is surrounded by a circlet of short ciliated tentacles in several rows. The peanut worm is both a burrower and a deposit feeder, and the water drawn toward the tentacles by the beating cilia carries minute organisms as well as sand and silt left over from construction of its tube. All this material is trapped in mucus and swallowed. The sexes are separate; emission of sperm by the males is said to induce females to shed their eggs, and fertilization takes place in sea water. A month later, the larvae metamorphose into young worms that settle to the bottom. Peanut worms contract quickly and must be narcotized before they are fixed and preserved by the collector.

Buried in intertidal fine sand or in muddy sand flats, and sometimes in similar substrata just below the low-tide line, live the curious hemichordates or acorn worms. The only species nearby, the colorful sixteen-centimeter-long *Saccoglossus kowalevskii*, makes its presence known by little piles of slightly coiled, easily recognized fine, ropelike castings. The U-shaped burrow can many times be further identified by its characteristic odor of iodoform. The wormlike body is soft, sluggish, very fragile, difficult to collect undamaged, and even more difficult to preserve whole. Acorn worms are easy to recognize by the whitish proboscis, the orange collar, and the long, beige trunk with easily visible paired gill slits along its entire length. The high-domed, somewhat conical proboscis within the collar resembles an acorn in its cup. Locomotor powers are limited, and the animals are sluggish. As acorn worms burrow through the substratum, they swallow sand with their microscopic fauna and flora, digest the organic matter, and pass the indigestible sand to the surface as a cast.

Their main interests to biologists lay in the idea, formerly accepted, that because of their unique larval development and the presence of some structures in the adult, they were thought to be a connecting link with the echinoderms (starfishes and sea urchins) on one hand, and with the vertebrates (phylum Chordata), the group to which we belong, on the other. The Hemichordata now have been removed from the phylum Chordata in most modern treatments, and have been given separate phyletic standing. In parts of the world where acorn worms are found in relatively large numbers, they are relished as table delicacies.

Bryozoa

Decorated with Sea Lace

W alking along the beach or in the lee of a jetty, especially after a storm, the observant beach stroller is quite apt to see a stone, shell, piece of solid flotsam, or seaweed, particularly kelp, washed up with one or more rounded patches of whitish, yellowish, or brick-reddish crust on its surface. If we pick this object up and look more closely, we can see that it is a hard encrustation, difficult, nearly impossible to remove by hand, and covered with regularly arranged, minute openings. Examining it with a hand lens, we find a colony of hundreds or thousands of minute individuals, each of the openings representing one animal or zooid with its species-specific (unique to the species) sculpturing, pores, spines, or other decoration. We have found the remains of the colony of a species of the phylum Bryozoa. The colony arose from one individual by budding, and because most of the first species observed were mosslike in appearance, the group received the name Bryozoa, which translates into "moss animals."

The individual members of the colony, the zooids, are minute, about 1/50 inch (0.65 millimeter) and are more or less cylindrical, boxlike, tubular, or vase-shaped in form, and sometimes polymorphic (two or more distinct-looking types of the same species occur in the same colony) in structure. The commonest type of nonfeeding zooid is the avicularium, which resembles a bird's head with raptorial (hawklike) beak, and which helps keep the colony clean by picking off unwanted material.

Avicularia that are stalked can bend and make rapid pecking movements, which enable them to defend the colony against small organisms, including the settling larvae of other sessile (attached) animals. Another kind of nonfeeding zooid, found in *Scrupocellaria* and other genera, is the Vibraculum. A long, bristlelike structure called a seta, the Vibraculum can be moved in one plane and sweeps away bits of detritus (debris

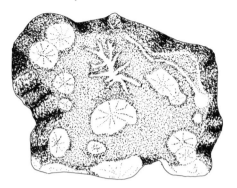

0.5 mm
(approx. ¹/₅₀ ")

Cryptosula pallasiana—Sea Lace. Forms orange to red hard-crusted thin to thick colonies on rocks. Zooecia have broad based horseshoe-shaped openings with small tooth on each side near base and front wall dotted with holes.

from wear) and settling larvae. Zooid modifications for reproduction are interesting but too complex to consider here.

The outer wall of each zooid most often is a supportive and protective layer that becomes an *exoskeleton* (external skeleton) when it is hardened by calcium carbonate. In this way it forms a rigid case, sometimes called a shell or test, within which are the soft parts of the animal. This case is called an ectocyst or *zooecium* (plural zooecia), and remains long after the animal dies and the soft parts have disappeared. These are the zooecia composing the colony that we find on the beach. To discover a living bryozoan colony, we would have to search on a submerged hard substratum or at least on one that was almost constantly covered with water. Colonies of bryozoa lacking calcium carbonate are soft, rubbery, gelatinous, membranous, or leathery, and do not affect us as beachcombing collectors because they deteriorate quickly out of water.

The soft parts of a zooid consist of the viscera and the tentacle sheath. The sheath houses the most unique organ of this group, the lophophore. It is a series of hollow, ciliated tentacles borne on a prominent, retractable, horseshoe-shaped ridge. In

Bryozoa • 83

the center of the lophophore is the mouth. The ciliated tentacles move a current of water, which ordinarily contains minute food particles, toward this opening. The digestive system is U-shaped and the animal has a true body cavity or coelom. The development of bryozoans involves a free-swimming larval stage, which, after living as a member of the zooplankton for a short time, settles on a suitable hard substratum and gives rise to the colony by asexual budding.

Species like *Bugula turrita*, instead of encrusting, grow up as fluffy orange, yellow, brown or beige, graceful, bushlike colonies, often twelve inches high, composed of spiral branches. The tufted, flat, fanlike branchlets terminate with rows of transparent zooids, whose anatomy we can see plainly through the walls. Species of *Bugula* are abundant from Maine to North Carolina, live mostly in shallow waters, and are particularly luxuriant on wharf piles and sea walls. Economically it is a particularly important animal as a fouling organism when its growth is abundant on ship bottoms and on docks. Its bulk can reduce the speed of the vessels as much as 30 percent; with it on the hull, tying up at boat slips is difficult. Worldwide, more than 130 species of bryozoans have been collected from the hulls of oceangoing vessels.

Other forms like *Aetea anguina* and *Bowerbankia gracilis* grow erect in separate, single-stranded zooecia, and can be seen without magnification as white, threadlike networks on seaweeds like *Laminaria* (Kelp), *Fucus* (Rockweed), and *Rhodymenia* (Dulse).

It is, however, the encrusting forms, common but difficult to accurately identify, which have given the common name, Sea Lace, to many members of this group. They grow on just about every substratum except sand and mud. One species, *Membranipora tuberculata*, is even commonly found on drifting *Sargassum* (Gulfweed). Along with members of the genus *Membranipora*, species forming colonies with lacy crusts in the geographic area we are considering commonly belong to the genera *Crisia, Conopeum, Electra, Callopora, Microporella, Cribilina, Smittina, Cryptosoula,* and *Schizoporella*. The crusts of the last two genera may be single- or double-layered, thin and flat or thick and irregular, and may be orange, red, brown, or purple instead of white. Among other encrusting genera are the interesting panpipe bryozoans of the genus *Tu-bulipora*, whose colonies are characterized by fused, tubular, open-ended zooecia, which when growing in relatively undisturbed deeper water become erect and branch much like antlers.

Together with hydroids (Coelenterata), bryozoans are considered among the most abundant marine epiphytic (living on plant surfaces) animals, probably being drawn to the surfaces of the algae by an attractant that the plants produce. Although they are highly successful in exploiting these and other hard surfaces, they compete constantly with other kinds of animals in different phyla for this living space. A few species of bryozoans even bore into calcareous substrata, but thus far the mechanism with which they do so has not been discovered.

No Bryozoa are known to be parasitic, although many species live communally with other animals or with seaweeds. The group is very ancient, occurring in the Late Cambrian and all subsequent formations. Earlier naturalists thought that members of this phylum were seaweeds, probably because of the bushy, thickly tufted *Bugula*. Though it was discovered in the seventeenth century that they were animals, as late as 1759, the great Swedish systematist, Carolus Linnaeus, grouped them with corals and hydroids. There they remained until 1830, when English zoologist, J. V. Thompson, recognized their unique characteristics and created the phylum Polyzoa for them. They received the name Bryozoa in the following year from the German zoologist, Christian Gottfried Ehrenberg.

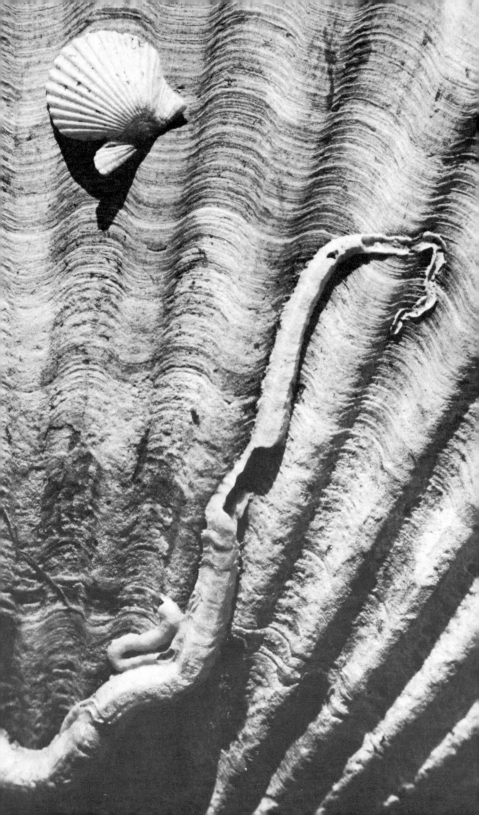

Annelida

Bait for Your Hooks

Astroll along nearly any breakwater or rocky outcrop on the North or Mid-Atlantic coast at the right time of year, in good weather or bad, will reveal a motley crowd of young and old people concentrating on the activity that many feel is more widely enjoyed than any other—fishing. If their bait is live, it is usually a specimen of the locally common "ragworm" or "clam worm," *Nereis virens*. Apart from earthworms, which are terrestrial and do not belong to the same taxonomic group, the worms most commonly used for bait here and off the Atlantic coast of Europe are believed to be the Lug Worm, *Arenicola*, and the Clam Worm.

Nereis virens occurs from south of New England, north along the coast of Labrador, through the Arctic to the northern coasts of Europe and Great Britain. In both Europe and in this country, it has been and continues to be a favorite experimental animal for the physiologist, the embryologist, the ecologist, and the comparative invertebrate anatomist.

Nereis is a segmented roundworm belonging to the phylum Annelida, and to the great class of marine worms, the Polychaeta (many bristles), and more especially to the so-called *Polychaeta errantia*. This name is used to separate, for the most part, the marine free-living, free-swimming, burrowing predacious polychaetes from the others. Polychaetes have distinct segments; all except the head segment have a pair of distinctive paddlelike muscular projections from the body wall, called parapodia (side feet), which are more complicated and more highly developed toward the center of the body. Motion, breathing, and sensitivity to touch are their functions. The blood-vessel-filled parapodia in *Nereis* have two easily distinguishable parts, both provided with a downward-pointing sensitive organ (cirrus), and golden-hued setae or bristles: the dorsal (upper) lobe or notopodium and the ventral (lower) lobe or neuropodium.

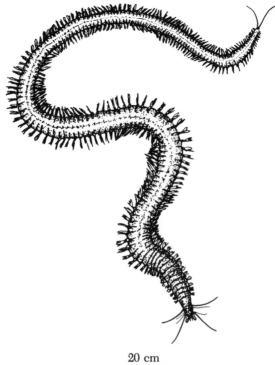

20 cm
(approx. 7⅛")

Nereis virens—The Clam Worm.

The head has special sense organs, consisting of two dorsal tentacles, a pair of ventral palps or taste organs, four eyes, and four sense organs around the mouth. The mouth has a reversible proboscis with a few sets of lateral spines, and ends with two dark-brown, cow-horn-shaped jaws that can bite vigorously on a plane parallel with the ground. Depending on the age and size of the worm, it may have as many as 200 uniform segments behind the head, the last one bearing a pair of trailing, short, stringlike sense organs. New segments are always added just in front of this terminal segment.

The Clam Worm is one of the largest, commonest, and most colorful of our marine worms. It grows to a length of 30 centimeters or more (width about 1 centimeter), and the iridescence of the greenish upper surface of the body gives the species its name, *virens*. They live under stones, or burrow in the sand or mud of sheltered bays where we can collect them either interti-

Annelida • 89

dally or just below the low-tide line. When disturbed or on the move, they swim vigorously in a serpentine motion, often playing the part of wandering hunters, and usually thrusting the proboscis forward to seize other worms or suitable prey with their powerful jaws. A clam worm can easily destroy creatures as large as or even larger than itself. Experimental work shows that no matter how well pieces of worms or clam meat are hidden, *Nereis* will find them. Clam worms therefore are common not only in clam flats but also in beds of the edible mussel.

Ricketts and Calvin point out that clam worms "are very active and squirm violently when captured, protruding and withdrawing their chitinous jaws. . . . Their powerful jaws are capable of delivering a businesslike bite to tender wrists and arms (and to the tender skin between the bases of fingers), but in collecting hundreds of them barehanded, we have rarely been bitten, always taking the precaution of not holding them too long."

Nereis lives in the sand in tubes whose casts are easy to recognize. The tubes are made by extrusion of a sticky mucus from lateral glands along the body. The mucus hardens quite rapidly, at the same time incorporating adhering grains of sand from the immediate environment. This flexible tube fits the worms so closely that, using their setae (bristlelike spines), they can move within it and out of it rapidly. Because their habit is to leave their burrows at night, they then become prey to fishes like the tautog and the scup, which prod them out of the sand.

Most marine worms apparently spawn in concert with tidal rhythms and with the amount of light reaching the sea, so that both the sun and the moon profoundly influence their reproductive activities. In this way, the nocturnal habit of *Nereis* swimming together in large numbers and in characteristic undulations presumably is connected with seasonal reproductive activity. The iridescent steel-blue and green males swim in groups inshore at low tide at this time.

At this time too, their appearance, together with that of the dull green, orange, or reddish females, changes so radically that these sexually mature forms were thought to be a different species, and were given the name *Heteronereis*, the term now used to denote the sexual phase alone. Berrill describes this stage: "As the season approaches, the posterior segments swell up with either egg or sperm, while the appendages normally used for creeping become changed into paddles for swimming. Then after midnight, in the dark of the moon during the summer months, the two sexes leave the sea floor and swarm to the surface of the water. Ripe males are white or gray where the sperm shows through the skin, while the back ends of the females are red with eggs. The eggs and sperm are shed into the water. When the process is over, the worms drop back to their accustomed place, and in due time grow new back ends since the old and exhausted segments usually drop off." The eggs are fertilized freely in the water, and the zygote (fertilized egg) develops into a typical larval stage called a trochophore. If it is not eaten by one of many potential predators, the trochophore, now a member of the zooplankton, metamorphoses, becomes wormlike, settles to the bottom, and grows into an adult *Nereis*.

Nereis virens has been discovered living in interesting association with other organisms. It is now known to be a secondary host for a parasitic fluke that lives in the intestinal tract of the common eel. Experimentally, it has proven a profitable animal to use in investigations of behavior. Fishermen claim that as bait, the clam worm has no rival for some kinds of fish, and most bait dealers usually have a good supply, stored on rockweed in a cool part of their stores. The mariculture of clam worms provides a surprisingly tidy income for many individuals of all ages living not far from tidal flats and rocky outcrops along the east coast of Maine. Clam worms are so popular with anglers that they doubled in price during the past few years; they are not difficult to dig, and are easily shipped and stored.

A Can of Sea Worms

The world of marine worms has been known as long as people have lived along the shores of salt water. For hundreds of years, all worm-shaped invertebrates were considered to be closely related. The first naturalists, and indeed

5 cm
(approx. 2″)

Pectinaria gouldi—The Gold Tooth Worm. The worm can be seen inside its ice cream cone-shaped tube of sand with its setae ("gold teeth") protecting the entrance.

many of their colleagues in later centuries, failed to notice the striking structural and environmental differences that warranted their being placed in distinct groups. So it is that the varied natural and artificial beaches and subtidal bottoms of the shoreline are inhabited by an unexpectedly large number of interesting species of unrelated groups of free-living worms. Perhaps the best-known New England worms living in the sediments washed by the tides are the polychaetes (Polychaeta), whose most economically important member, the iridescent Clam Worm, *Nereis virens*, reaches a maximum length of about eighteen inches and is much sought as bait by coastal fishermen.

Polychaetes live in sand and mud flats, and once you are familiar with their tracks and trails, you can collect them with relative ease. Worms, being soft-bodied, self-destruct easily; narcotize them with fresh water or Epsom salts or refrigeration, and then preserve them with 7 to 10 percent neutral formalin. Worm burrows may be distinguished from other holes in the sand or mud by their characteristic piles or casts of material, their conical sunken depressions or elevated cones, or the presence or absence of bits of detritus incorporated in tubes barely extending above the sand surface.

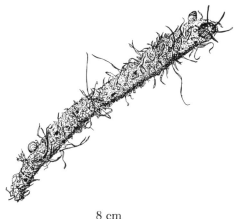

8 cm
(approx. 3⅛")

Diopatra cuprea—The Plumed Worm. Head of the worm may be seen extending slightly from the part of the parchment tube incorporating bits of detritus, which extends from sand surface.

It is not always easy to dislodge a burrowing worm. Those living in long, relatively deep tubes may be able to descend as fast as we can shovel. They or their tubes may be easily broken or fragmented, or they may disappear altogether if the substratum around the dug hole caves in. The Plumed Worm *Diopatra* lives in long parchment tubes into which it weaves camouflaging bits of shell, seaweed, and other debris. Press the shovel quickly into the sand close behind the tube of this animal, with as little mechanical disturbance to the substratum as possible, and grasp the now-unearthed tube containing the animal immediately underneath to keep the worm from rapidly escaping.

Polychaetes are close marine relatives of terrestrial earthworms and fresh- and saltwater leeches, and together with these other two groups form the segmented round worms that belong to the phylum Annelida. Rings around their bodies, both internally and externally, separate annelids from all other worm groups. Polychaetes typically have paired, bristlelike appendages on each segment (Polychaeta means many-bristled), and along the sides of the body are fleshy, paddlelike lobes, filaments, or other paired structures that may be used for swimming, burrowing, or respiration, depending on the spe-

Annelida • 93

cies. The bristles have a great variety of shapes and are often used to distinguish one species from another. Polychaetes live in many ways; most often as tube dwellers that trap and filter their food, and sometimes as nomadic predatory animals feeding on other soft-bodied creatures. Nearly all have combinations of tentacles, antennae, cirri (slender small projections), and palps concentrated near the anterior end that provide acute senses of taste and touch, and most polychaetes have at least one pair of these structures on the roof of the head. Sexes are usually separate. Eggs and sperm are shed freely in the water, sometimes in response to temperature change, but often cyclically in tune with the tides. The eggs hatch into larvae, which drift with the currents for days before settling to the bottom and metamorphosing into adult worms.

The crawling polychaetes living beneath stones and shells on the large algae, and in communities of sessile organisms such as mussels and barnacles, include such forms as *Nereis virens*, the Clam Worm, and its close relative, *Nereis limbata*; *Cirratulus* with its long, threadlike filaments that function spectacularly as gills; and the scaleworms, *Harmathoë* and *Lepidonotus*, with their peculiar dorsal, paired, platelike scales. The burrowers like *Glycera*, the Beakthrower; *Lumbrinereis*; *Ophelia*; the capitellids; *Arenicola*, the Lug Worm; and the magnificently colored *Cirratulus*, the Fringed Worm, all move through the sand or sand-mud substratum by peristaltic contractions.

Polychaetes live in varied ways; many have become tube dwellers. Among these are the carnivorous worms, such as *Diopatra*, the Plumed Worm that incorporates fragments of its environment in its membranous three-foot tube; *Clymenella*, the Bamboo Worm, which lives head downward intertidally in delicate sand tubes; the beautiful Fan Worms or Feather Dusters, including such common forms as *Sabella*, *Potamilla*, *Hydroides*, *Serpula*, and *Spirorbis*, which build either straight tubes of sand grains and mucus or uniquely shaped calcareous tubes attached to different kinds of surfaces. *Pectinaria*, the Mason or Gold-Tooth Worm, which builds delicate-appearing but sturdily formed tubes in the shape of ice cream cones, is commonly found in many of our sand flats, as is one of the most beautiful of our coastal worms, *Amphitrite ornata*, and the phosphorescent, creamy-white Parchment Tube Worm,

Chaetopterus, which lives in a two-foot-long, U-shaped tube of self-manufactured parchment, often with a species of the symbiotic Pea Crab, *Pinnotheres*, keeping it company.

Another group of common but far less-known marine polychaetes are the possibly primitive archiannelids, tiny worms that live mostly intertidally on or between sand grains, in mud, or among algae. They differ structurally from the polychaetes mostly in having very few setae (bristles), few or no parapodia and other appendages, and external hairlike cilia that enable them to glide on and through their tortuous habitat.

Animal behaviorists have found some polychaetes particularly useful in studying associations between animal species belonging to widely separated groups. Demorest Davenport discovered puzzling alliances involving sharing of food between scaleworms including *Harmothöe* and echinoderms, including starfish, brittle stars, sea urchins and sea cucumbers. One species of starfish was found able to release enough chemical attractant into the surrounding water to stimulate the approach of the polychaete from quite a distance away. It was also found that wounded or dying echinoderms had a repellent action on the scale worms, sparing the polychaete a relationship that would yield no food. Additional studies in this field indicated that one species of polychaete was a willing partner (commensal) with thirteen kinds of animals belonging to four phyla, and that different species of small scale worms live with some forms of tube worms, presumably sharing the food of their large, fat, soft cohabitors. A classic case of commensalism occurring between *Nereis* and some species of hermit crabs was investigated by inducing both the worm and the crab to accept an artificial shell of glass. R. V. Gotto writes that it was then observed that the polychaete *Nereis*, which normally occupied the upper whorls of the shell, would glide forward when the crab was feeding, seize a bit of food from the crab's mandibles, and quickly retreat with it to the depths of the shell.

Crustacea

Barnacles—The Clinging Crustaceans

*T*he Barnacle, a ubiquitous and cosmopolitan, exclusively marine crustacean, is one of the most obvious and numerous kinds of animals found along our shores. It encrusts intertidal and subtidal rocky headlands, pilings, breakwaters, rocks and boulders, living and dead shells, and even animals such as horseshoe crabs.

Barnacles are sometimes thought of as mollusks because their bodies are entirely enclosed within calcareous plates, yet their morphology during embryonic and larval development, together with their paired, jointed appendages, reveals them as true arthropods belonging to the class Crustacea.

The cirruslike or feathery feet of its better-known representatives give these marine animals the name Cirripedia. Several groups of true barnacles (order Thoracica) are readily distinguishable: the Lepadomorpha or stalked forms, to which belong the goose-necked barnacles; the widely known Balanomorpha or common rock barnacles, gray barnacles, and ivory barnacles all often called acorn barnacles because of their resemblance to the acorn; the less widely distributed Verrucomorpha, smaller and more symmetrical than the acorn barnacles; and the three orders of curiously adapted, chitin-clothed barnacles most of which are parasitic on or within several kinds of invertebrate hosts, including blue and horseshoe crabs and certain tunicates.

Scientific investigation of barnacles has a distinguished and interesting history starting with the Greeks, some of whom believed that geese were spawned spontaneously from a stalked variety called goose-necked barnacles. Probably the best-known investigator was Charles Darwin. Immediately after he returned to England from the famous voyage of the *Beagle* that furnished him so much material for his publications on evolution, he spent seven years producing monographs on recent and fossil barnacles. *A Monograph on the Sub-Class Cirripedia*

1 cm
(approx. $^7/_{16}''$)

Balanus balanoides—The Common Rock Barnacle. The largest individuals on the rock are a year older than the smallest.

(1851–1854) is a classic and is still the basic reference work for cirripede specialists.

Louis Agassiz described common acorn barnacles as "nothing more than a little shrimp-like animal standing on its head in a limestone house and kicking food into its mouth." Permanently attached to a solid surface by its head, it has neither the eyes nor the sensory antennae found in more typical crustaceans. The six pairs of appendages (comparable to the locomotory limbs of other crustaceans) act as a unit; the protective valves, uppermost on the calcium carbonate skeleton, separate, and the feathery legs are thrust out, swept through the water, and drawn back inside the valve, carrying the entrapped plankton and detrital particles inside the body. This action is repeated every few seconds.

The characteristic method of reproduction in all barnacles is hermaphroditism, and although each individual has both sexes, cross-fertilization is the rule. Fertilization takes place when the slender contractile sperm tube of one barnacle is thrust through the shell valves into a neighboring barnacle. Within the parent, the fertilized eggs develop into typical motile crustacean larvae, which after hatching become free-living members of the zooplankton for a few weeks. Here they metamorphose into the larval stage, which eventually attaches to a suitable hard surface after using principally their sensory antennae to explore and test the area for a place for attachment. The larva employs a sticky cement secreted by an antennal gland to attach itself, and soon thereafter a calcium carbonate skeleton is started at the base and sides.

As the animal grows, the six or eight exoskeletal calcium carbonate plates are slowly enlarged by accumulating additional material, and at the same time the covering of the protected internal soft parts of the body is molted or shed into the surrounding seawater. The molted skins are extremely light and usually wash about in the water for a long time before settling. Swimmers seeing these suspended in the water for the first time nearly always think they have discovered a new or rare animal.

Few of the intertidal barnacles are larger than a third of an inch in diameter, and may be an inch high if they are crowded together in large numbers. Smaller still are some of the parasitic forms. The largest barnacles live at some depth off the western coast of the United States, growing to a height of up to nine inches, a diameter of four inches, and a weight of more than half a pound. Barnacles often add color to their environment, ranging from white, yellow, pink, orange, and red to purple with occasional striped forms.

Some kinds of barnacles always live in the littoral zone below the low-tide line; others are found at greater depths; still others live only intertidally and are able to stand temporary exposure at low tide; and finally, some forms are adapted for living in the spray zone at high tide on wave-lashed rocky shores. Acorn barnacles can withstand exposure when the tide is out because of the wall of limey plates enclosing the base and body circumference, and by the pair of valves on top, which can be most completely sealed when necessary.

The numbers of individuals in an area can be enormous. Examine the rocky shores along any headland and you will see thousands of these animals per square meter. This kind of supercrowding tends to induce smothering, and together with the competition sometimes offered by other sessile organisms kills many barnacles. The barnacles higher up on the shore grow slowly and live about five years; the faster growers farther down may die after three years. In an intertidal area the smallest barnacles invariably are the youngest.

Among the acorn barnacle's enemies are snails such as the dog whelk. Starfishes are also found on barnacles when more attractive food is unobtainable. In their planktonic larval stages they are subject to predation by the larger zooplankton and by different kinds of fish.

As efficient fouling machines, barnacles make a costly nuisance of themselves on ship bottoms, lobster pots, and marine hardware. Before antifouling paints were available (their efficiency against settling barnacles is partial at best), ships had to carry as much as 300 tons of these organisms. Large accumulations on hulls sharply reduce the ship's speed, increase fuel consumption, and cause frequent and costly docking. Barnacle fouling costs the shipping industry in this country more than $100 million annually.

The barnacle–human relationship is not all on the red side of the ledger, however. In Chile, Charles Darwin reported that the soft parts of the barnacle were considered a delicacy and were an esteemed ingredient in soups and chowders. Waldo Schmitt, late dean of American crustacea specialists, said "The flavor—all its own—of this barnacle soup, as I can attest, is equal to that of the best clam chowder, while the flesh is more palatable than clam meat." One kind of goose-necked barnacle is sometimes used for food on the coasts of Brittany, Spain, and Italy, and the giant West Coast barnacles are eaten by the Indians.

Callinectes sapidus,
A Favorite Target of Homo Sapiens

O ne of the handsomest, liveliest, and most delectable animals to grace the bottoms of the shores, estuaries, and bays of New England is the colorful Blue Crab, *Callinectes sapidus* (*sapidus* comes from the Latin *sapio*, meaning tasty or savory). Together with the other edible crabs, shrimps, and lobsters, this arthropod belongs to the Decapoda or ten-footed crustaceans, the most highly developed order of the class Crustacea.

Superficially, a Blue Crab seems very different from a lobster or shrimp, but when the folded and flattened abdomen is opened out, we can see a relatively close relationship. Among the common characteristics are the hard-shell covering of each of the nineteen segments, which make the jointed protective exoskeleton, and the thin, soft intersegmental areas between, which allow mobility.

The crab's appendages display much structural variety: the toothlike mandibles are used to cut up tidbits presented by the outer, limblike mouth appendages, and the ten pairs of appendages following them, Stebbing says, have the functions of "tasting and pasting, biting and fighting, grasping and clasping, walking and a kind of inarticulate talking, swimming, burrowing, besides the automatic services which they render to the eggs in the brood pouch and to the animal's own respiration." With so many units to work with, the crab has almost any tool it needs. The fifth pair of legs, of which all the segments are broad and flattened like paddles, is used as oars. These swimming legs enable the Blue Crab to propel itself rapidly through the water, easily outdistancing its close relatives, which have to get about as best they can by running along the bottom.

The Blue Crab and its relatives can throw off their limbs and grow new ones (autotomy), a provision that must provide a good method for escaping from enemies. Spasmodic contraction of muscles in the second joint enables partition to take place. The nearly colorless blood coagulates quickly, and the wound closes rapidly. A new limb begins to grow at once from

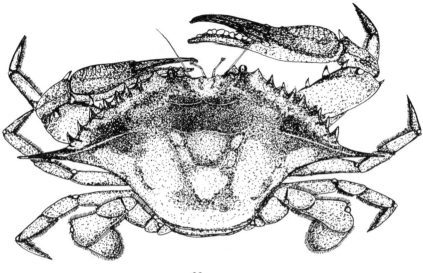

23 cm
(approx. 9")

Callinectes sapidus—The Blue Crab.

a bud beneath the scar, and after a few molts it closely resembles the original leg.

Because of its armorlike casing, which is incapable of expansion, the crab can grow only by shedding this inelastic housing. The shedding is called molting, and a black, white, or red line down the back of the crab indicates that the animal will molt within the next few days. In this condition, the crab is known to the fisherman as a "peeler." During molting, the posterior part of the body protrudes through a gap made by cracks in each side of the shell. It takes about fifteen minutes for the crab to free itself completely by rhythmic throbbing. Then it becomes the table delicacy known as a soft-shelled crab. Forty-eight hours later the new shell is quite hard. Ordinarily the crab eats its discarded shell and thus regains the calcium carbonate needed to harden its new housing. Molting occurs every few weeks while the crab is young; later, shedding may take place no more than once a year. At the time of molting or shedding, the Blue Crab is nearly defenseless and cannot eat, which is the price these animals pay for their protective armor.

The sexes in blue crabs and in all other decapods are separate; the larger male crab, commonly about seventeen centimeters wide, has a sharply pointed abdomen, and the female's abdomen is well rounded. After copulation, the female stores sperm until the eggs are ready to be deposited. She carries the eggs cemented in bunches to hairs on her swimmerets; the larger the crab the more eggs she carries; 50,000 to 2,000,000 eggs are not an uncommon burden. In this condition, a crab is said to be "in sponge." The eggs hatch directly into the sea water, and eventually settle to the bottom and metamorphose into the adult form. All the larval stages are spent floating about as members of the pelagic zooplankton, subject to the predations of carnivorous plankters and small fish. Very few of the tens of thousands of larvae originally released by one female ever grow to maturity.

The Blue Crab, one of the largest crabs on the Atlantic and Gulf coasts of the United States, ranges as far south as Uruguay. It sometimes penetrates from the ocean into fresh water, and indeed, before our estuaries became polluted, it was most abundant in the brackish waters of our area. Pollution may also explain today's low Blue Crab population, for most mating occurs in waters of low salinity. The females do return to waters of relatively high salinity before the larvae hatch. Blue crabs feed on many kinds of living plants and animals (they are quite destructive to beds of small steamer clams and other thin-shelled bivalves). Their main food, though, seems to be dead animals, and blue crab traps or "pots" are customarily baited with dead fish. Watch out: crabs can strike with their large specialized first pair of walking legs (chelipeds) by suddenly thrusting them outward and closing down hard with the pointed tips of their viselike claws. The painful bite seldom does more than draw blood. Avoid it by grasping the crab between the bases of the swimming legs by thumb and forefinger.

The crab's stalked compound eyes are controlled separately, and can be laid back into sockets in the shell at the front of the head when mechanical or other injury threatens. Passing a shadow across the eye is enough stimulus to trigger this protective reaction. The eyes probably form no more than a very crude image, but are exceptionally good in determining both the movement and the location of an object.

Blue crabs have several enemies other than man. They are hunted along the shores and in shallow water by gulls and herons, and in deeper waters they fall victim to octopi and to fish with teeth sharp enough to crush them. The Blue Crab, like the Lady Crab and the Cancer Crab, retreats to deeper offshore waters during the winter months.

The blue crabs were once economically important in southern New England; unfortunately, contamination of their environment in bays, estuaries, and marshes has reduced their once large, commercially valuable harvest to a pitiful few, and they have disappeared entirely from many areas. But they still sustain fair-sized populations elsewhere along the Atlantic Coast. The Blue Crab fishery off the Chesapeake Bay region alone yielded a catch of more than 48 million pounds in 1983. The total value of this Blue Crab fishery was $17,104,646. Fresh Blue Crab prices go through extreme swings at your favorite fish market because of their highly seasonal production and poor storage qualities. They must be kept alive until cooked, and the fresh-cooked meat has a short life, a few days at best.

Proper preparation of the Blue Crab for the table is an outstanding achievement in *haute cuisine*. Experienced trenchermen often associate it with a beautiful painting, a prize-winning novel, or a breathtaking musical composition. Do we need more reason to cleanse our inshore waters than to bring the Blue Crab population back to its former prominence?

The Old Shell Game—
A Matter of Life or Death

With practiced beachcomber's eye, as we splash along just below the tide line of a sand flat or protected beach, we will often spot the scuttling activities of one of three species of shell-carrying crabs, commonly known as hermit crabs. Found not only in New England waters, it is also abundant along the water's edge from Maine to Florida, living on

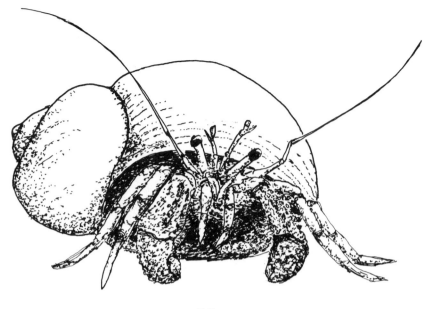

5.5 cm
(approx. 2¼")

Pagurus pollicaris—The Large or Warty Hermit Crab. This individual is living in the shell of a moon snail.

pebbly, sandy, and muddy bottoms, in tide pools, behind sandbars, and in other shallow, relatively unexposed areas.

The outstanding visible feature of the Hermit Crab is its shell, but, of course, the shell is not part of the crab's body; it belonged to a snail that had died before the crab found it. The shell protects the soft, unprotected rear end (abdomen) of the crab. This part of the animal is curved in a spiral that conforms to the shape of the snail shell. In taking a shell, the crab first explores it thoroughly inside and out with claws and feet, probably to make sure it is not occupied, and then with surprising speed it makes the change from its current shell to the new one.

In the southern part of New England, hermit crabs use the empty shells of snails and whelks. They favor those of periwinkles, dog whelks, dove shells, and mud snails. Apparently it is less the type of shell that is important to the crab than its size and availability. As the crab grows, the dead shell must be discarded for a larger one. If, after moving into its new house, the shell proves unsuitable, the crab immediately changes back to its old home and again takes up the search for new housing. Sometimes a crab will find a shell that for some reason seems eminently suitable but is occupied by another crab. It will make an attempt to dislodge the other crab and capture the shell for its own use, usually in a lively fight. Crabs first move into a shell after they metamorphose on the bottom into their adult forms from their planktonic larval existence. These almost microscopic hermit crabs easily find a shell to appropriate from the multitude of minute shells lining the bottom of the littoral sand flats.

Because the body of the Hermit Crab is a spiral that fits the central spiral column of the shell, it is very difficult to remove the animal from the shell by pulling it. The last pair of appendages on the abdomen are in the form of a clamp, adding to the crab's ability to maintain its position in the shell.

Hermit crabs are mostly scavengers but are also known to be carnivorous and even cannibalistic, if they see the opportunity. Very often one crab coming upon another that is too slow in getting into a new shell will kill and eat its temporarily defenseless relative.

As in other crabs, the eggs are fertilized before they leave the body of the female. As the eggs are extruded by the female they are attached to small appendages of the tail by a sticky proteinaceous material that she produces. Because of the spiral curve of her body, though, they are cradled on the left side of the abdomen, not in the center as in other kinds of crabs. The eggs are often brilliantly colored in shades of orange or dark purple. When danger seems past, the crab will often come far enough out of her shell to wave the egg masses, aerating and cleaning them at the same time. She also emerges at hatching time and nudges off the young with a setose (brushlike) appendage on her left side.

Male hermit crabs are usually larger and much more pugnacious than females, and ordinarily fight spiritedly and often for the favor of the more desirable females. After beating down the opposition, a male will probably drag the shell of a female until she is ready to shed. Then he immediately deposits his sperm inside her shell and onto her abdomen, ensuring fertilization of the eggs as they come out.

Ecologists and others interested in animal associations observe that shells occupied by hermit crabs often seem unusually suitable settling places for other organisms. One species of hermit crab is always found with a sea anemone attached to its shell. The anemone's broad base is wrapped around the shell, with its mouth, surrounded by tentacles, on the underside next to the shell opening. Presumably the anemone affords protection to the hermit, and in return shares in gathering up the bits and pieces from the hermit crab's meals. When the hermit crab moves to a new shell, it detaches the anemone from the old shell with its chelate (pincerlike) claws and places it on the new shell. In this partnership, though, the hermit crab doesn't always have to move to a larger shell as it grows, for the enveloping and similarly growing anemone may extend beyond the opening of the shell, increasing the size of the hermit crab's home. As time passes, the anemone may dissolve the shell, enveloping the hermit crab in a soft, fleshy mantle that is actually part of the anemone's body.

In another association the smooth, rounded yellow lumps of a common local species of sponge dredged from a few fathoms of water may have a round opening in which we can see the claws of a small hermit crab. When we cut the sponge open, we find the body of the hermit crab resting in a spiral cavity at whose apex are the remains of the shell, which has been dissolved by the sponge. The latter had originally settled on it and then replaced it with its own tissues.

Often, hermit crabs have colonies of small hydroids, particularly those of the genus *Hydractinia*, attached to the shells they carry, giving the shells a velvety appearance when the hydroid individuals are expanded. These species of hydroids may also be found attached to rocks and to seaweeds. When *Hydractinia* colonies are carried by hermit crabs, though, they always develop an additional type of spiral zooid (individual), which is thought to be protective.

Other organisms that may settle on hermit crab shells are barnacles, flattened limpet types of mollusks, algae, and others. No special types of relationships have been observed between these occasional and often chance settlers and the hermit crabs.

Zoologists interested in investigating animal behavior have paid close attention to the biology and activities of hermit crabs, and a sizable literature is building about these active and apparently always busy little animals in research libraries. Many Italians give such investigations a more personal and practical touch by cooking the crabs in oil. When done they are served in the shell and taken out with a pin or a toothpick to be eaten.

And Other Crabs

*B*arring the shelled mollusks, probably no animal is more typical or more suggestive of the seashore than the crab. Even the dining-room zoologist, who knows animals only as gastronomic delicacies, is familiar with the Blue Crab. For the naturalist, *Callinectes sapidus* has another appeal. Out among its haunts in the saltwater bays and inlets, clinging idly to a tangle of seaweed or lording it along the sandy bottom over its less well offensively endowed fellow invertebrates, the Blue Crab is a colorful object that attracts immediate attention.

The Blue Crab is strikingly handsome, but the Lady Crab can be called, without stretching the word, really beautiful. The Lady Crab, *Ovalipes ocellatus*, has a velvet costume of delicate greenish-yellow flecked with red and ornamented with peacock eyes of closely stippled purple dots. The dorsal shield is gracefully rounded, the claws symmetrical and nicely proportioned, and the last pair of legs fashioned into oval swimming plates that add grace to its appearance and serve it well in its aquatic habitat.

As animals with such striking coloration often are, the Lady Crab is found on or close to sandy beaches, spending much time in the shallows, and on occasion parading over the exposed area of shore. More often, it buries itself partially in the loose sand, its stalked, darting eyes always on the lookout for prey or intruders. Sometimes the Lady Crab ventures out from the shore and swims rapidly over the surface of the bottom just beyond the low-tide line.

5 cm
(approx. 2″)

Carcinides maenas—The Green Crab.

When disturbed out on the beach, it cuts a furrow into the sand with sharp oarlike flippers and sinks out of sight. The Lady Crab disappears so rapidly that it is difficult to believe an animal with this shape can dig out of sight instantaneously. This burrowing habit is very useful for all marine animals that venture on exposed beaches. By sinking into the sand, they are protected against the crashing breakers during a storm.

The Lady Crab is expert at catching small fishes. A school of minnows flashes by. There is a dart of eager claws and the fishes pass on less one of their number. The captive is disposed of head first, and the Lady Crab sinks back into ambush with only its alert knobby eyes protruding on their long stalks.

Wanderers along the seashore often notice *Carcinides maenas*, an olive-green crab sometimes mottled with yellow or red, and with a comb of ten teeth along the front of the dorsal shield. Called the Green Crab, it is found in both brackish and saline habitats, and is at home on the other side of the Atlantic as well as along the New England coast. Because it is so active and pugnacious, the French call it *le crabe enragé*. Confined

110 • Crustacea

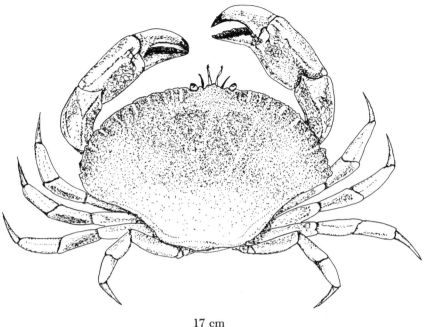

17 cm
(approx. 6¾")

Cancer borealis—The Northern or Jonah Crab.

with other species, he often runs amok and indulges in wholesale slaughter, yet when his mate is about to shed her protective armor, he will stand guard over her. An interesting sight is to come upon a hard-shelled male crab clinging to its soft-shelled partner and protecting her during the molting period, when she is quite defenseless.

If you are so unfortunate as to be gripped by the crushing pincer of a Green Crab, try to forget the pain by musing that the creature probably is exerting a pull of about two kilograms, a force equivalent to nearly thirty times the weight of its own body. The average hand grip of a man is capable of a fifty-kilogram pull, about two-thirds of his own weight. If a man had as much relative strength in his grip as a crab, hand-clasping as a sign of friendship would soon be prohibited.

Somewhat similar in appearance to the Green Crab are the various species of small mud crabs, olive-brown, with large powerful claws often tipped with black. To this group belong several closely similar species of the genus *panopeus*. They

Crustacea • 111

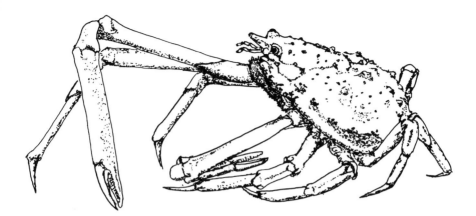

12.5 cm
(approx. 5")

Libinia emarginata—The Common Spider Crab.

abound in muddy localities, under stones, and hiding among masses of sponges, seaweeds, discarded cans, and other artifacts. Mud crabs are for the most part quiescent, lounging in a protected environment, lethargically living and letting live. When uncovered or detected under a stone, they either remain motionless or arouse themselves and scuttle away.

A large and noticeable coastal crab is the Rock Crab, *Cancer irroratus*. Its shell, which grows to be five inches wide, is yellowish, thickly stippled with reddish dots, and bordered along the forward edge with nine blunt teeth. It has a broad body and heavy claws. This crab lives in the shallow water close to the shore and, when the tide is out, can often be found under stones, in rocky crevices, or buried in the sand or gravel. Though edible in the winter months when they molt, their flesh is not as delicate or as highly esteemed as that of the Blue Crab.

Heavier and more massive than the Rock Crab, but quite similar in appearance, is its relative, the Jonah Crab. The dull, brick-red color and stony texture give the crab a look of power and hardness. Enormously rugged but stubby claws add to the impression of strength. Relying on its size, its toughness, and the strength of its black pincers, it does not often seek shelter. Boldly clinging to a ledge or point of rock, it resists the waves.

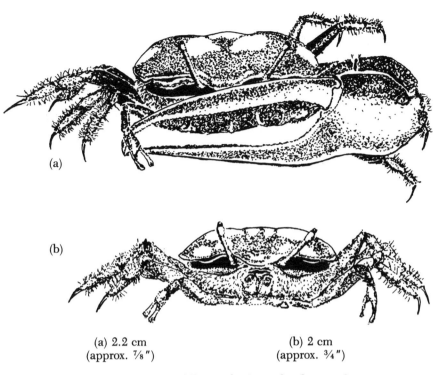

(a)

(b)

(a) 2.2 cm   (b) 2 cm
(approx. ⅞")   (approx. ¾")

Uca pugnax—The Fiddler Crab. (a) Male. (b) Female.

Along with us, its greatest enemies are the herring gulls and great black-backed gulls that wheel and scream along the Atlantic coast. These voracious birds carry off many a bold Jonah to satisfy their large appetites.

The Jonah Crab is no swimmer, and neither is the Rock Crab. Both crawl along on their pointed legs, progressing sidewise as all true crabs do, pulling with one set of legs and pushing with those opposite. In spite of their awkward appearance and bow legs, they cover ground at a fair pace.

Cancer, the ancient Greek name for crab, is the generic name of both the Rock and Jonah Crab. The former is *Cancer irroratus*, "the besprinkled one," and the latter is *Cancer borealis*, the "cancer crab of the North." In mythology, Cancer was the crab commissioned by Juno to plague Hercules when he was in the Lernean swamp battling its fierce denizen, the many-headed serpent. Hercules, however, crushed the crab with a single blow. Juno, in her queenly way, "knighted" the crab by placing it in the evening sky, where it is a constellation visible to anyone with imagination.

These large, active, colorful crustaceans are a striking contrast to the scrawny, slow-moving, cosmopolitan, omnivorous Spider Crab—*Libinia dubia*, with six small spines down the center of its back, and *Libinia emarginata*, with nine spines in that position. They are like caricatures, having humpy, bulging, toad-shaped bodies with skinny legs, and emaciated claws. Spiders they are in having long, slender legs, but they seem so weak and sluggish that here the comparison ends.

Spider crabs are prodigious gatherers of an organic "moss," and therein probably rests their salvation. Their bodies, covered with chitinous hairs, become coated with a bacterial or diatomaceous ooze that encourages the growth of larger algae, as well as hydroids, tube worms, and other marine invertebrates. This coating can be an excellent camouflage, protecting the crab from predatory neighbors.

The Spider Crab passively encourages the growth of a marine garden on its carapace, and it is frequently the gardener who plants the vegetation there. This crab has been observed to snip off bits of sponge, sprays of *Bugula* (a low, branching bryozoan), hydroids, or even fronds of seaweeds and actually place them on its back, head, or legs. The cut ends are first touched to the mouth, smeared with oral cement, and then glued on or caught in the fine hairs that mat its dorsal surface. When the Spider Crab changes its environment, it may modify its makeup in tune with its new surroundings.

This masking habit or camouflage has been studied by zoologists interested in animal behavior. It is a device undoubtedly used in defense, but it seems equally important as an offense strategy, enabling the crab to steal up to its prey unnoticed or to lie in wait for it unseen. The dramatic march of Birnam Wood on Dunsinane happens daily on the bottoms of our marine embayments, where spider crabs and other invertebrates stalk their prey.

Spider crabs are very numerous in our shallow marine ponds, and may be found often in large numbers along the upper bottoms of bays and inlets. They wander slowly about the bottom on their stilt legs, loiter in underwater prairies of eelgrass, or poke in the crannies and crevices of disintegrating litters of pelecypod and gastropod shells. Shedding individuals cling to the tops of clumps of *Zostera marina* (eelgrass) close to the surface, a surfacing phenomenon that may be connected with their molting.

Out in the deeper waters of our sounds such as Vineyard, Rhode Island, Block Island, and Long Island, the spider crabs are also very abundant. Oyster fishermen dredge them up in immense numbers. It is not unusual for local fishermen, while removing starfish from the floors of these waters, to trap large numbers of these crabs. When caught in this way, neither the females, some burdened with huge clusters of orange eggs, nor the larger males offer much resistance to handling. Thrown overboard, they sink like stones to the bottom; they cannot swim.

Off the coast of Japan and other lands bordering the North Pacific Ocean lives a giant spider crab, the largest of all crustaceans. With legs outspread, it can span as much as twelve feet. This huge crab seems like a myth, yet its spindly, weak legs furnish much of the canned crabmeat sold as "king" crab. Its body never exceeds a foot in length or breadth. Though frightening in appearance, it is apparently no special menace to the fisherman in whose lines it occasionally becomes entangled.

Most New Englanders who are fond of eating oysters and mussels have come across the very small pink crustaceans that sometimes add a touch of color to the oyster stew. These are *Pinnotheres maculatus*, the Pea Crabs: curious, sluggish, pillow-shaped crabs no larger than a garden pea. In the Northeast, they usually live commensally (in partnership) with oysters (oyster crabs) or mussels (mussel crabs), and in the tubes of both the Parchment Tube Worm, *Chaetopterus*, and the Ornate Worm, *Amphitrite*.

In other parts of the coastal United States species of pea crabs live in the tubes of a variety of worms; some cohabit in the burrows of the Mud Shrimp; some inhabit the gill baskets of large sea squirts; some live on the under surface of Cake

Urchins; still others dwell in Paper Clams and Keyhole Limpets. Many species of crabs have their own species of host.

Pea crabs are not harmful, and in several parts of the world they are considered great delicacies. They have relatively small legs, rudimentary eyes, and are one-half to one inch across. The female Pea Crab lives safely housed between the gills in the mussel or oyster mantle cavity—one crab to one shellfish. The mantle cavity is really part of the outer surface of the animal, although it appears to be internal. This space contains the gills and foot of the shellfish. The crab cannot leave because when she is mature she is too large to escape from her adopted home.

The male is a minute, typically wandering, rounder, free-swimmer in a hard black shell. Their mating was a mystery for many years, until it was observed that the smaller male enters the living bivalve host of the female, mates with her, and then moves on to repeat his performance elsewhere. She produces fertilized eggs and carries them in the usual way until they hatch and are released to the surrounding seawater, where the pea crab larvae become temporary members of the zooplankton.

Interestingly, in metamorphosis, the body structure of the first crab stage is modified and becomes structurally adapted for reaching the host with the incoming current of water that brings the bivalve its food and oxygen.

According to the observations of G. E. and N. MacGinnitie, who put glass windows in the shells of a mussel and were able to watch the activities of pea crabs, they "obtain their food by eating some of the mucous string by means of which the mussel carries food to its mouth." More commonly they are thought to take their food from the incoming food supply of the host mollusk.

Some zoologists believe that a Pea Crab is a true parasite, because while it is in the host, its body appears to degenerate, becoming far softer than when it first invaded the bivalve, and its power of locomotion seems to decrease. There is also evidence that while *Pinnotheres* is in the mantle cavity of its host, the latter's gills, palps, and other structures may erode.

In the U-shaped parchment tube of the large marine worm, *Chaetopterus*, a very small crab, *Pinnixia chaetopterana*, lives commensally with the worm. The worm builds a recurved tube nearly two feet long in the sand with both ends open and projecting just above the surface, a few inches apart. The bend of the tube is roomy and swollen, but the openings are so small that neither worm nor crab can ever make their escape. Using its own secretion, the worm surrounds itself with the tube and thus becomes a prisoner. The crab, which entered the tube when it was a larva and then metamorphosed into an adult, grew too large to escape.

We are naturally gregarious animals, and perhaps for this reason great congregations always arouse our interest. So it is that fiddler crabs by sheer numbers take our attention.

Above the high-water line and between tide marks, in salt marshes, on mud and sand flats, or where tall spartina grass grows in stiff, green spears, fiddler crabs riddle the sand with burrows. Along the margin of the beach when the tide is out, a horde of little crabs will scuttle away when disturbed, retreating shoreward to hide in muddy crevices or to seek the safety of their one- to two-foot-deep tunnels. Very often these crabs scurry in droves so large among the grassy clumps and thickets that the rustle is audible.

A quick look reveals two groups of crabs, those with two small front claws and others bearing one small and one extremely large claw. The former are females, the latter males. The males have the habit of slowly waving the large claw back and forth. The fancied resemblance between this activity and that of a bowing bass viol player gives it the name "fiddler." The great claw, usually on the right side, is strictly a weapon for defense. The crab eats with the small claw, picking up with it bits of algae; its burrow is dug with the walking legs. When coming out of its tunnel, the giant claw appears first, and when it is retreating into the burrow the claw enters last.

The mud flats in which fiddlers live are punctured with innumerable small holes, entrances to their burrows. In excavating, the crabs scrape together large pellets of mud and sand, bringing them out of the tunnels and scattering them far from the entrances. The smaller pellets strewn about profusely in the same area are fecal droppings. Although fiddlers do not eat the sand, it is assumed that they sift the grains with their mouth parts, picking out the nutrient materials mixed up with it.

Uca is the generic name of the Fiddler Crab. In our waters the three species are: *pugnax*, "the fighter" (common in salt marshes); *minax*; and *pugilator*, "the threatener," largest of the three and usually farthest from the salt water, frequently living where the water is brackish.

Hippa talpoida, the Mole Crab or Sand Bug, is a small, cylindrical beast, light brown to white tinged with purple, which lives sometimes in large numbers between the tide lines on open beaches. The male *Hippa* lives buried from sight and so is rarely seen by summer visitors to the seashore. To see these crabs, we must dig into the exposed sand near low-water mark.

Hippa is only about an inch long. Its body is smooth and barrel-shaped, its legs short but fashioned into sturdy instruments for burrowing, which it does very swiftly by pushing backward and downward into the sand. A help in the burrowing is the specialized, elongated, triangular, shovel-shaped telson. Without the powerful claws of other crabs, and having soft and small mouth parts, it lives by swallowing large quantities of sand. The internal organs extract the large numbers of minute animals and algae that live in the interstices between the sand grains.

The Mole Crab has a remarkable pair of plumed and pliant antennae. Each has more than a hundred segments, each joint bearing a fringe of eight to twelve long hairs. The crab generally holds these delicate plumes concealed under its body, where they are thought to be used for cleaning particles from other organs and appendages. They probably have some sensory function as well. Its plumose feet prevent the crab from sinking too rapidly when the beach floods.

Together with the Blue Crab and the Hermit Crab, these are probably the marine crabs found in greatest numbers along our shores.

Freshwater Shellfish Delicacy

The common Crayfish, Crawfish, Crawdad, or Crab, as they are variously known, are the only true freshwater decapods found near the coast in rivers, large and small, as well as in many lakes and ponds. They live best in streams that course over limestone somewhere along their upper reaches and in the ponds into which the streams empty. They appear in this guide because their shells may sometimes turn up at the heads of estuaries.

The structure and behavior of the Crayfish is remarkably similar to that of the Lobster, but it differs in its development by having no free-swimming larval stages, and by being only four to five inches long. The adults can live out of water for weeks if they are kept moist and cool; however, the natural means of dispersal of Crayfish are very limited, the eggs being carried by the female. When hatched, the young have all the appendages of the adult except two pairs of abdominal structures.

Some species have become adapted to almost terrestrial habits. A number of them in the United States are often found quite far from open water, burrowing in the damp meadows, their burrows reaching down to the water table. Other kinds erect chimneylike piles of mud at the mouths of their burrows, and in places like these their chimneys are so numerous that not too long ago, they were said to "hamper farming operations by interfering with the harvesting machines, clogging and ruining them!"

Male and female adult Crayfish are easily distinguished: males usually have larger claws and narrower abdomens, and the minute cuplike genital opening is found on the base of the fifth pair of legs rather than at the base of the third pair as in females. At one of the lower joints of all the walking legs is a "breaking point," where the Crayfish when grabbed can break off its leg. Missing legs are nearly always regenerated.

Body color varies from dark brown through red, orange, green, and, rarely, blue, with shades between. Usually, newly molted specimens are more brightly colored than older specimens. Their color generally varies with the background of their substratum.

Crayfish are omnivorous, preferring succulent aquatic plants to animal food (which they prefer live or freshly killed). Adults usually remain hidden under stones and other bottom debris in waters from three to five feet deep during the day, but between dusk and dawn they come out and feed. When it is cloudy, and when streams are shaded, they may leave their hiding places and wander about during the day.

Crayfish live in many ponds and streams, and it is suspected that as many more species of native crayfish could be found as there are kinds released from the bait buckets of bass fishermen. Surprisingly, no survey of the crayfish of Rhode Island has been made, although much is known about these decapods in some neighboring states. All, though, are equally delicious when prepared for the table.

Crayfish may be collected with long-handled dip nets, minnow seines, minnow traps, and by examining overhanging banks, masses of vegetation, and the undersides of submerged logs and stones. Best results are often obtained by hunting them at night with a headlamp (a flashlight with a headband).

Lobster Lore: The American Lobster

Tis the voice of the Lobster: I heard him declare,
"you have baked me too brown, I must sugar my hair."
— Lewis Carroll, *Alice in Wonderland*

The popularity of the American Lobster, *Homarus americanus*, as a table delicacy the length and breadth of boreal North America, must be responsible for the boundless interest in this crustacean's life and times. Research on its biology, distribution, and value in the marketplace is matched by study of its culture and commercial development by individuals and shellfish firms. The best known and most informative monograph on the biology of the Lobster by F. H. Herrick in the first decade of this century, *The Natural History of the American Lobster*, was the first of a whole shelf of publications on this most important food crustacean. The annual Lobster catch not many years ago was more than 100,000,000 individuals, but is now much less for many reasons, including overexploitation and increased efficiency in methods of collecting and inadequate limitation and enforcement of catches. At today's prices, lobsters are luxury items.

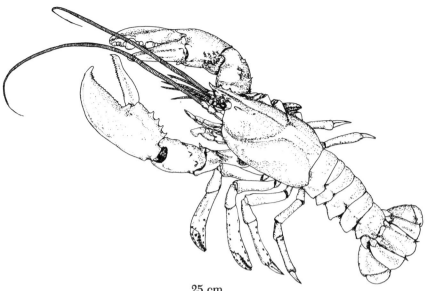

25 cm
(approx. 9⅞")

Homarus americanus—The American Lobster. The average length of the adult lobster collected for the market is 25 centimeters (.45 to .65 kilogram) although offshore specimens weighing more than 20 kilograms have been captured.

Travelers to the southern United States and to the Caribbean islands may be confused by the "spiny lobster" listed on menus. *Panulirus argus* is a very different animal from *Homarus*. It is smaller, has spines all over its body, and lacks the powerful claws of its northern relative; only its muscle-filled abdomen is eaten.

Homarus lives in rock ledges and crevices and along rocky bottoms the length of the New England coast and as far south as Virginia, in the entrances to the larger bays, in many of the sounds, and in other waters with suitable depth and sufficient food. Ordinarily it is a dark greenish or reddish purple, although very occasionally a striking light blue or green lobster is caught in a trap or speared by a scuba diver. All turn bright red when boiled or when they are preserved. Lobsters are scavengers, and will feed on all manner of organic matter, from seaweed to dead fish; lobster fishermen take advantage of the latter taste when they bait their traps or pots. Live food, including the softer-shelled bivalves (clams and mussels), is also

Crustacea • 121

acceptable, as are bones of fish and parts of clam shells, but the lobster's relatively slow movements rarely enable it to capture a very active animal like a small bottom fish. Their main enemies appear to be people and codfish. The lobsters in this area seem to be divided into two size groups. The smaller ones live near the shore at shallow depths, and the larger ones—up to 45 pounds and more—are collected by draggers in deeper waters offshore. With commercial lobstering endlessly increasing the pressure, the average overall size of both groups of lobsters has decreased. Investigations by the Narragansett Marine Laboratory at the University of Rhode Island indicate that the small coastal lobsters may be a race separate from that of the giants that live at 200 fathoms.

The Lobster gives us an excellent example of an animal with an outer or exoskeleton (shell), compared with an animal like us with an inner or endoskeleton (bones). The exoskeleton protects the internal organs and the other soft tissues, and its lining is the rigid attachment area for the body muscles. Also, the hard shell makes possible a jointed armor with legs, claws, and other appendages. Because the shell is inelastic and will not accommodate growth, it has to be molted or shed for the animal to increase in size. As it molts, an ever-widening split occurs along the top of the abdomen (tail), and the Lobster lies on its side, bends its body in the shape of a V, backs out slowly, drawing along all its soft parts, and crawls away to hide until its new shell is hardened. During this period, its soft mouth parts prevent it from eating. Just before the shell hardens, the growth substances absorb water quickly and the body expands, depending on how well it has fed. When the shell is molted, toxic wastes produced by the body are discarded at the same time.

The common way of getting about is walking, using the four pairs of legs. The Lobster walks deliberately and carefully, sensitively divining obstacles with the forward-waving antennae. Lobsters can also swim after a fashion, when sufficiently provoked or when they are away from protective outcrops of the substratum. In swimming, they flip their tails forward violently and are shot backward precipitously.

The Lobster sexes are separate, and in mating, the hard-shelled male impregnates the soft-shelled female within a few hours after she has shed. The sperm remain viable in the body of the female for at least nine months, until she spawns. In spawning, the eggs flow from openings in the female's body over the receptacle on her body where the sperm are stored. The eggs are now fertilized, and are then attached to the mother's swimmerets by a natural adhesive, and here they remain protected and aerated throughout an incubation of ten to eleven months. A Lobster lays from 3,000 eggs (7-inch female), to about 10,000 (10-inch female, 1¾ pounds), to about 75,000 (18-inch females). Females carrying eggs are known as "berried" lobsters. When newly hatched, the larvae are planktonic (floating), and go through several molts in the two months before they settle to the bottom. Young lobsters remain inshore during the summer, and with cold weather, migrate into deeper water.

The one-pound Lobster is called a "chicken" lobster even though it may be as much as six years old. It takes about five or six chicken lobsters to make one pound of lobster meat. Lobsters weighing more than two and a half pounds are called "jumbos." On the proper method of boiling a lobster, opinions differ. Many believe that the tenderest meat is produced by placing a live lobster in a roomy container, covering it with cold tap water, adding one tablespoon salt, boiling for five minutes and simmering for several minutes more, depending on its size. An alternate method is to steam the lobster for fifteen minutes, with a little water in the bottom of the pot; this method gives a less soggy lobster that's even tastier.

The Native Shrimp

*F*ew coast dwellers are aware that in parts of their bays and salt ponds, and especially in embayments lining the shore, are pockets of small varieties of deliciously edible shrimp. Although these animals are neither present in marketable quantities nor nearly as large as the commercially available "pink" and "brown" shrimp, they are plentiful enough for canapes or salads.

Shrimps are arthropods in the class Crustacea and subclass Malacostraca, and belong to a well-defined and equally well-known order, the Decapoda or tenfooted crustaceans. This order includes crayfish, lobsters, and crabs. Like their fellow decapods, shrimp have a segmented external skeleton made mostly of chitin, with thin and softer jointed areas that permit the parts to move backward and forward; nineteen true appendage-bearing segments or somites; stalked eyes; and a posterior terminal telson. The laterally compressed (narrow) body is divided into three main regions, the head, thorax, and abdomen, of which we cannot tell the first two apart because they are coalesced and are covered by a dorsal shield, the carapace. Though built on a uniform structural plan, the paired, segmented appendages have become adapted to different functions: the first two are the feelers (antennules and antennae); the third pair, just outside the mouth, are the jaws (mandibles); the fourth and fifth pairs are accessory jaws (maxillae); the sixth through eighth pairs are the so-called jaw feet that assist ingestion (maxillipeds); the next five pairs of appendages are the walking legs, one or more pairs of which may be clawed; the following five pairs of appendages on the abdomen are the swimmerets (pleopods); and the last pair of appendages are the uropods, which, together with the telson, form the tail-fan. With so many units so varied in design, we can see why decapods are able to become involved in many activities.

One of the more startling aspects of decapod biology is the ability to cast off a leg and grow a new one in its place (autotomy). Limb regeneration is well known in crabs and lobsters, but has not been well documented in shrimps. Because a new limb ordinarily becomes indistinguishable from its predecessor after a few molts, molting is indispensable in the life history of a Shrimp. The hard shell of the Shrimp cannot expand, and if the animal is to grow, it must shed this suit of armor periodically. It does so by backing out through a transverse slit along the posterior part of the carapace, shedding not only the shell but also the lining of its stomach and the terminal part of its intestinal tract. Molting is not only dangerous and exhausting for the decapod, but it also exposes the individual to its natural predators. Ordinarily, shrimp eat their shed exoskeleton, presumably deriving the lime salts needed for rapid hardening of

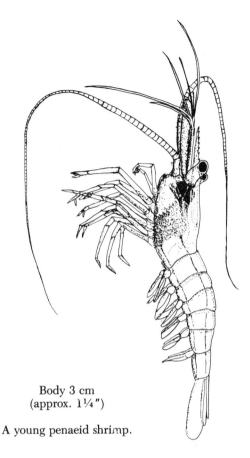

Body 3 cm
(approx. 1¼")

A young penaeid shrimp.

the new shell. Between molts, shrimp eat almost anything, including algae, small crustaceans, worms, larvae, and small fish, and sometimes they apparently are excellent scavengers.

Because the exoskeletons of the small local shrimp are semi-transparent, we can see through the carapace the more or less elliptical, bulbous heart. It is easy, and fascinating, to see the rapidly beating heart of a native shrimp after we catch it and put it in a small, clean glass jar of sea water.

As we expect in active animals, the sense organs of shrimp are well developed. Each of the antennules has three branches, which are constantly in motion searching the immediate environment. The two long branches extend the entire body length, and sometimes farther. The antennae are about half the length of the body, and are ordinarily trailed backward along the sides. The eyes are noticeably large and are carried on movable stalks. The pointed and sometimes spined forward extension of the carapace between the eyes is the rostrum, a structure of considerable diagnostic significance.

Like all other decapods, shrimp have separate sexes. The external opening for the passage of sperm is near the basal segments of the last pair of legs in the male; in the female, the eggs come from gonoduct openings near the bases of the third from last pair of legs. The female often has a special organ, a sperm receptacle, in which she stores the sperm from the male until the eggs are ready to be deposited. Females in most species of shrimps carry the eggs after extrusion on their swimmerets, each egg being cemented with material associated with the covering of the egg. A female shrimp "in berry" (carrying fertilized eggs) may carry 2,000 eggs. They hatch as a special kind of planktonic larva, the zoea, which later metamorphoses to the adult. Soon after the eggs have hatched, the female molts; sometimes she may spawn twice in a season. Most berried females travel seaward before their broods hatch. Here again, placing local egg-carrying female shrimp in a clean glass jar with sea water will reveal in its amazing entirety and color the developing egg mass. Some of the smaller species of shrimps change their sex as they grow, being first male and later female.

Shrimps and prawns are able swimmers, as anyone knows who has tried to net them. When alarmed, they can move rapidly backward by folding the tail-fan under the abdomen and suddenly flipping it. Ordinarily they swim forward by means of the five pairs of abdominal swimming legs with bristles on the inner edges, locking each pair together as though holding hands. Some shrimps characteristically walk along the bottom, using only their last two pairs of legs. When they are swimming, the five pairs of swimming legs beat in graceful rhythmic succession. In the fall, as the temperature begins to drop, many species move to deeper water, where they remain until the following spring when the water starts to warm up.

Although both are in a subgroup of the decapods, the Natantia, shrimps differ from prawns. "Prawn" is a name for the larger kinds of swimming shrimps, and "shrimp" refers to all smaller types. In general, the body of a shrimp is flatter than that of a prawn when we see it from above, its right and left limbs are more widely separated, and it lacks a prominent *rostrum* (front extension of carapace).

Three of the many kinds of shrimps along the Atlantic Coast, many of them with unusual habits, are usually common in waters from Maine to Cape Hatteras. *Hippolyte (Virbius) zostericola* is a smaller, translucent shrimp, mottled greenish and brown, sometimes spotted with red, sometimes entirely green, living, as the species name indicates, in or close to patches of eelgrass. One of the obvious identifying marks, along with its color, is the sharp, almost perpendicular bend of the abdomen at the third segment. *Zostericola* ranges from Vineyard Sound in Massachusetts to the southern coast of New Jersey, and we can collect it by running a fairly coarse dip net through patches of eelgrass.

Palaemonetes vulgaris is the common prawn. The adults are much larger than *Hippolyte*, and are translucent, with brownish spots. It also occurs in eelgrass, but more often lives in ditches, salt marshes and similar places, frequently being found over mud-sand bottoms. It is distributed along the Atlantic Coast from New Hampshire southward.

Crangon septemspinosus, the most abundant of the three shrimps, is a translucent pale gray animal with minute star-shaped dark spots. It is found from Labrador to North Carolina, its numbers diminishing toward its southern limit. This is the common Sand Shrimp, a decapod usually numerous on sand flats and deeper water-sand sediments farther offshore. It has also been collected from tide pools. It is a relatively hardy combination of scavenger and carnivore that lives well in a marine aquarium. Its translucent grayness is a beautiful camouflage when it is resting motionless on the sand bottom, or partially buried in the sand. This and related shrimps change color with numerous chromatophores, which are under hormonal control, the hormones being produced in ductless glands in the eyestalks. When caught intertidally on an ebbing tide, it may be found burrowed several centimeters into the moist sand. Stomach contents of bluefish, flounders, striped bass, and other fishes frequenting its habitat show that the Sand Shrimp is among their foods.

Although they are most common south of the Virginia capes, we eat so many *Penaeus setiferus*, the White Shrimp, and the two other penaeids, the Pink Shrimp and the Brown Shrimp, that we can't ignore them here. They live mainly on the bottom during the day but swim upward on very dark days or at night. They are the shrimps in the freezing compartments of grocery stores and supermarkets, the most important market species of shrimp. In 1971 the United States catch of these "Pink" and "Brown" shrimp was roughly 234 million pounds (heads-off weight), worth about $166.2 million to the fishermen who landed them, and easily the most valuable fishery in the United States.

Recipes for preparing shrimp are as delicious as they are numerous. The smaller species of shrimps from the coastal waters may be used for nearly all.

Orchestia, The Sand Dancer

. . . after prolonged examination of homologous parts [of Amphipods] the observer would not be so much impressed with the difficulty of a common descent as with the intrinsic simplicity of the processes by which these wonderful differences of structure might have been produced. For if a son may be taller than his father, a daughter stouter than her mother, in the same family one child have straight hair and another curls, one brother be smooth and the other a hairy man, variations of a corresponding kind suffice to explain the most striking dissimilarities that the Amphipoda can furnish. Lengthen or contract a limb, make a joint tumid or flatten it out, multiply the spines or prickles, narrow or expand the body, or so treat one part of it at the expense of the other, let it be cylindrical or depressed or laterally pinched, stiffly outstretched or coiled into a ball,—by such differences as these, in regard to which many species present the most minute transitions, it will be found that genera and families are separated, without the least necessity or reasonableness of attributing to them other than a common origin.

—Thomas R. R. Stebbing, 1888

.8 cm
(approx. ⅜″)

Orchestia agilis—The Sand Hopper, Sand Flea, or Beach Flea. After a night of feeding on dead material thrown on the shore by the tide, the beach hopper excavates a burrow above the high-tide line in which it will spend the following day.

O n many of the cobble-free strands of our shores, if you are an observant beach stroller walking down the beach slope toward the water, you may find, near the row of cast-up seaweed that marks the high-tide line, little openings in the dried sand about five millimeters in diameter. Carefully probing these holes, you will find that those not made by air escaping from the sand when it was last washed by a flooding tide are probably the burrows of species of amphipods known collectively as Sand Fleas.

The name Sand Flea or Beach Flea demonstrates misleading nomenclature, the use of common names for ubiquitous animals. These marine beasts have nothing but their hopping in common with the insects called fleas. They are semiterrestrial crustaceans belonging to the Amphipoda (considered to be the most modern and most recently evolved of the higher orders of crustacea), family *Talitridae* (genera *Orchestia*, from the Greek meaning dancer), and *Talorchestia*. They are more properly called Sand Hoppers. They feed mostly on decaying seaweed and are harmless.

Crustacea • 129

Sand hoppers are most abundant under piles of rotting sea-weed left high on the beach by high tides, and it is in these long rows of mixed species of dead and decaying algae that they get their food. After a night of scavenging and feeding on dead plant and animal material cast ashore by the tide, for which they will often make special trips from above the high-tide line to the water's edge, the Beach Hopper excavates a burrow in the sand on the dry upper beach. On the following night it will abandon this shelter, feed again, and dig a new burrow.

The burrows are built head first. As it excavates these tempo-rary structures, *Orchestia* looks like a digging dog, bracing itself with its second and third pairs of legs while the gnatho-pods push the sediment rearward to the back appendages and spiny tail fan, which then spray it into the air. Final work on the burrow utilizes a cementing secretion produced by small glands all over the body that enable the Beach Hopper to firm the burrow lining with sand.

Other amphipods live among the grasses and other flora of salt marshes, and relatives of *Orchestia* such as the Side-Swim-mer, *Gammarus* (Greek for lobster), are abundant just below mean low water under stones, shells, and similar substratum cover.

The body color of the Beach Hopper, resembling the sub-stratum on which it rests most often, may be olive-brown or green to gray, white, or translucent. Posteriorly, the animal may be bluish, and the antennae may range from red to red-brown. *Orchestia* is widely distributed along the entire Atlan-tic Coast of North America, and *Talorchestia* from the Bay of Fundy to Cape Hatteras, and is also found in coastal Europe. The body is strongly compressed from side to side. Part of the population of beach hoppers in an area may be subtidal, if only during dispersal of their young in the water column, a habit that we can use to advantage. We can either shake tidal drift algae stacked at the high tide line over a clear spot on the beach, picking the animals up individually, or we can dunk the seaweed in a nearby tide pool, stimulating the *Orchestia* to swim out freely and climb up on our legs, from which we can easily pick them and put them into a container. They will preserve best in a five percent formalin-seawater mixture.

You may have the sensation once in a while of being bitten when you pick up a Beach Hopper, but look closely at the suspected bite and you'll find nothing more than slightly reddened skin.

The appendages in amphipods are similar in structure, and are arranged efficiently for their varied uses. Behind the two pairs of antennae in front of the mouth are the mandibles, maxillae, and clawed prehensile gnathopods that help in feeding and in burrowing, immediately in back of the mouth; then come five pairs of thoracic walking legs, to the first three pairs of which are attached the gills or respiratory organs; followed by three pairs of abdominal appendages adapted for swimming and three pairs of short, stiff appendages used as leaping organs. These animals seldom swim, walking with the walking legs, making faster movement over the surface with all the abdominal appendages. The animal leans far over to one side while it sculls or darts rapidly over the sand, aided by strong, pushing strokes of the telson (tail). The vigorous jump of the sand hoppers is set off by the sudden backward extension of abdomen and telson: a two centimeter *Talorchestia* can spring forward more than fifty times its own length, a feat said to be unequaled by any other animal its size. At times, beach hoppers are numerous enough in one place to look like small clouds when mechanical disturbance provokes them and they all jump into the air at once.

Although they live out of water, sand hoppers have kept their gills. Because these structures are smaller than those of more aquatic amphipods like the closely related *Haustorius*, the air must be humid for respiration to take place. Beach hoppers are limited for that reason to the moist sand that lies beneath the drifted seaweed, or to similarly damp areas. Beach hoppers react negatively to light and come out to feed only at night, another adaptation that keeps them from dessication.

Little has been written about reproduction in beach hoppers. It is known that the males differ morphologically from the females, and, further, that in the many species in the genus *Gammarus*, a related but aquatic form, the smaller females carry the larger males around on their backs for days before the molt that precedes the quick transfer of sperm. Next, the pair separates, and the eggs are released into the brood chamber on the underside of the body of the female and fertilized by the previously deposited sperm. A clutch may have from 2 to 750 eggs, and several broods a year are possible. The young remain in the brood chamber (marsupium) until it is cast off by the female at the next molt. The freed young closely resemble their parents.

L. Pardi describes a very interesting experiment demonstrating that these amphipods have a kind of "compass sense" in using their eyes to ascertain the sun's altitude, the plane of polarization of light in the sky, and the moon's position, together with some sort of internal "clock," to find their way to the level of the beach where they live. It has also been shown that under natural conditions, as when removed from tidal wash and placed just above the water line, they can regain the locality high on the beach from which they came by quickly recognizing features of their original habitat, including the skyline, and then rapidly jumping toward it.

Thomas Roscoe Reed Stebbing (1834–1926) was the first to work out many of the important subtleties in the systematics of amphipods, and his two major works (1888–1896) on the taxonomy of this group are still necessities for the specialist. Of these, his monograph on the amphipods collected during the voyage of *Challenger*, the landmark expedition marking the start of oceanography nearly a hundred years ago, was his major work. According to E. L. Mills, "it stands as a monumental piece of scholarship and a major source of reference."

The Horseshoe Crab—A Living Fossil

*F*or more than 300 million years, since the Triassic Period, horseshoe crabs identical with those touring the shores of our bays have struggled from the sea. They belong to one of the oldest known living varieties of creatures—so old that their only close relatives are animals that have been extinct for millions of years. They are known to zoologists as living fossils.

Anyone who has spent much time swimming in harbors or collecting quahogs, steamers, or mussels knows the Horseshoe

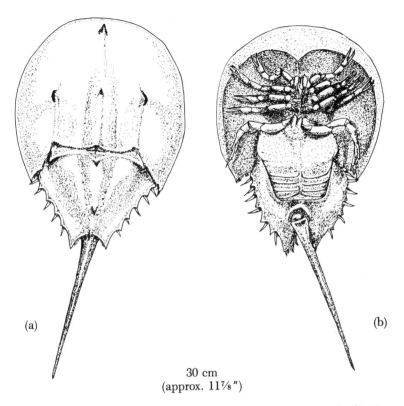

(a)   (b)

30 cm
(approx. 11⅞″)

Limulus polyphemus—The Horseshoe or King Crab. (a) Dorsal. (b) Ventral. This ancient relative of the spider (it is not a crustacean) lives in shallow water along the shore where it burrows in the sand and mud and eats worms and other small animals.

Crab, *Limulus polyphemus*. One of nature's most successful animals, it is a broad, flattish, dark creature with a long spike tail. Turned over, its shell rim looks like a perfect horseshoe. Although people are often alarmed when they inadvertently step on one of them while wading, the horseshoe crab is harmless.

Continents have shifted. Ocean bottoms have become mountain ridges. Nearly everything on earth has been altered while horseshoe crabs churned along apparently changeless, skirting ice ages and outliving geologic catastrophes. In scrambling geography, nature split the horseshoe crab population into two sections, one ranging the Atlantic Coast from Mexico to Maine, and the other living not on the American Pacific Coast but along the coasts of Southeast Asia.

Aristocrats are said to consider themselves bluebloods, but the Horseshoe Crab is literally a blueblooded animal. Human beings and other mammals have red blood because iron (in haemoglobin) is used in conveying oxygen in the blood stream. The Horseshoe Crab, like crustaceans and most mollusks, has copper (in haemocyanin) instead of iron in its blood. Horseshoe Crab blood turns blue when exposed to oxygen.

But blood color is only one of the many curious differences between the Horseshoe Crab and even its closest relatives. After all, it isn't every creature that uses its legs to grind its food, can't eat without walking, and has a mouth near what we consider the center of its chest.

As with nearly all arthropods, growth occurs by molting; the animal escapes from its exoskeleton through a slit that develops around the front and side margins of the large shield-shaped part of its body. After the Horseshoe Crab has completely squeezed forward from its shell, the old shell closes up almost completely and looks essentially like a living animal. Completely grown females are up to 20 inches long; the males are always shorter. It is thought that the males do not molt after becoming mature. The eggs, larvae, and adults are quite hardy and can be shipped alive for long distances. Because they are hardy and because adults can survive for weeks without food and water (if their gills are moist), these animals are particularly valuable to the experimental invertebrate zoologist.

The Horseshoe Crab has crushing teeth in the form of short, closely set spines on the large upper joints of each of its five pairs of legs. As it travels along the ocean floor, with the rim of its shell shoved under the mud, bulldozing like a snowplow, the ten leg bases push together and grind small mollusks, algae, worms, and other organisms gathered with the front pincers. After grinding, the toothed basal leg sections pass this masticated material into the mouth, which is near the center of the undersurface between the third and fifth pairs of legs. The operation is like the interdependent movements of an automatic machine, in that the animal cannot eat unless it is moving.

The long spinelike tail or telson may be moved in many directions because of its ball-and-socket attachment to the abdomen. It is used chiefly as a lever to help the animal right itself when it gets overturned. The horseshoe-shaped shield protects it from other animals, and because the flange is kept embedded in the sand it keeps the animal from being upset by waves. *Limulus* moves by combined walking and lurching. The four pairs of similar legs lift the body from the ground while the fifth pair, larger than the rest and ending in oddly constructed "pushers" that keep them from penetrating the sand but at the same time provide purchase, gives the body a violent shove forward. The fifth pair of legs, the telson, the hinged abdomen, and the movable spines along the sides of the abdomen act together in clearing away sand, silt, and mud during burrowing. This activity is amazingly rapid for an animal that seems clumsy. Horseshoe crabs can swim, but they do it awkwardly, and upside down.

Along the outside of each of two prominent lateral ridges at the back of the shield is a fairly large eye. Two small eyes are farther forward, one on each side of the less prominent median ridge. The structure of these eyes is quite different from that of the compound eyes of insects and crustaceans. A recent study reveals that *Limulus* can orient itself by sensing the plane of polarization of light. It also has five light-sensitive organs beneath the shell.

The Horseshoe Crab differs radically from the true crabs. For one thing, crabs have eyes on stalks, and the horseshoe's eyes are set in its head. No other creature grows a complete new set of lenses for its eyes when it sheds its shell. Also, the unique respiratory apparatus attached to the ventral side of the abdomen, consisting of six pairs of gill-books (they look like a book's gathered pages), differs radically from those of a shrimp or a lobster, and we can compare them with the swimming appendages beneath the abdomen or tails of these animals. On the dissecting table, the Horseshoe Crab, separated from its distinctive shell, looks more like a scorpion than any other known living animal.

Through the years, classification of the Horseshoe Crab has kept scientists arguing. For a century, it was lumped with such crustaceans as crabs and lobsters. In 1829, though, a German scientist pointed out that *Limulus* (some zoologists insist on the scientific name *Xiphosura*) was not at all similar to other crabs. He argued—as many still do today—that nothing now living is even remotely related to the Horseshoe Crab. Now it has been assigned to the arachnids, in company with the spiders, mites, ticks, scorpions, harvestmen, and similar beasts.

Female horseshoe crabs deposit about 1,000 eggs in each nest. They may return to the beach as many as ten times in the spring, laying more than 10,000 eggs. The nest apparently is chosen haphazardly. The female scuffs out a hollow in the sand, deposits the eggs usually at or just below the mean high-tide line, and the clinging smaller male then quickly deposits sperm on top of them. The mass of eggs is covered with sand, which is smoothed by waves at the next tide. Ordinarily the laying season begins late in May, and continues to July.

The tiny greenish, leathery-capsuled eggs—twelve of them measure about an inch—hatch in July or August. The miniature horseshoe crabs crawl out of the sand and head immediately for the shallows, where we may find them on sand or mud flats exposed at low tide. They are replicas of the parents, but lack the spike tail and are known as "trilobite" larvae because of their close but superficial resemblance to these extinct Crustacea. The first three years of their lives are the most dangerous because of predation by fish and gulls. The survivors continue to molt, and mature between ages nine and twelve.

Commonly the adults harbor accidental associates such as barnacles, jingle shells, tube worms, marine algae, and slipper shells that may settle nearly anywhere on the upper or lower surfaces of the larger anterior horseshoe-shaped part of the animal. More intimate associations are formed by ectocommensals (living on the body surface), such as the large cafe au lait-colored flatworm (Turbellaria), *Bdelloura*, which lives between the book gills, using the cuticle (hard skin) of these organs as a substratum (base for chemical action).

Collected in large numbers, horseshoe crabs have been used extensively as fertilizer and as chicken feed on farms, particularly along the northern part of the Atlantic Coast.

The Horseshoe Crab has helped in making several recent major discoveries in medicine that have saved many human lives. Unlike human blood, which contains several types of cells, Horseshoe Crab blood has only one type of cell, an amebocyte. The amebocyte contains large amounts of an enzyme called *Limulus* amebocyte lysate (LAL), which is very sensitive to pyrogens, the toxins produced by many pathogenic bacteria. Medical researchers can now use LAL for diagnosis; the test takes only an hour to produce results, and is far more sensitive than other methods, which take up to several hours. It is also far less expensive. The pharmaceutical industry sees promise in LAL for work in quality control. Today, LAL helps diagnose spinal meningitis, is a help in the study of blood-clotting mechanisms, and determines how severe several kinds of water pollution are by helping pinpoint the bacterial populations that are responsible.

Horseshoe crabs are not usually fare for gourmets, although the musculature is an esteemed delicacy in parts of the Middle Atlantic states.

Echinodermata

Dollars in the Sand

*T*he flat, thin, nearly circular skeletons of a curious group of echinoderms that we sometimes encounter between tidelines on the outer marine beaches are commonly known as sand dollars. The name was acquired because of their fancied resemblance to that now rare American coin, the silver dollar. They belong to the phylum Echinodermata, from the Greek words for hedgehog and skin, indicating that these are "spiny-skinned" animals. This division of animals contains the closely related sea stars, brittle stars, sea urchins, sea cucumbers, and the ancient sea lilies.

The Echinodermata have skeletons constructed of calcareous plates with spines that are more or less embedded in the skin: in sea cucumbers, these plates are loosely scattered, and the body is flexible; in sea stars and brittle stars, the plates articulate and the skeleton is somewhat pliable; whereas in sea urchins and sand dollars, the plates are fused and sutured together, forming a boxlike, immovable protective shell or test.

One of the most distinctive characteristics of echinoderms is that all have radial symmetry (a spokelike arrangement of parts around a central axis, as in jellyfish, anemones, etc.), compared with the bilateral type of symmetry (the individual can be divided into equal and opposite right and left halves), commonly encountered in other metazoans, including ourselves. This design is especially clear in sand dollars, where the upper (aboral) surface has a starlike pattern of five petal-like figures radiating from a central disk-shaped sieve plate (the madreporite), the entrance to the unique locomotory vascular system. These petal-shaped regions on the aboral surface are the areas perforated by the animal's respiratory apparatus. The underside (oral surface) has five relatively prominent, equidistant channels (the ambulacral grooves) emanating from the central mouth. These grooves unite with similar, less clearly defined structures on the upper surface and pass strings of

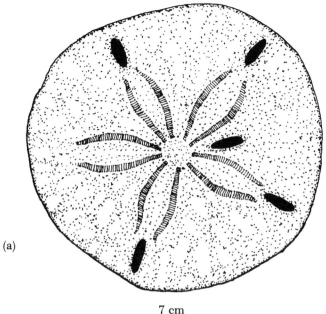

(a)

7 cm
(approx. 2¾ ")

Sand Dollars. (a) *Mellita quinquiesperforata*—The Keyhole-Urchin, common in shallow southern Atlantic waters. Upper side.

mucus containing food particles toward the mouth. The anal opening is at the edge of the test.

The Northern Sand Dollar, *Echinarachnius parma*, ranging from mean low water to about eighty fathoms, from Long Island Sound northward, is about three inches in diameter and has no openings in its test, whereas the slightly larger Southern Sand Dollar, or Keyhole-Urchin, *Mellita quinquiesperforata*, which is normally found from Cape Hatteras to the West Indies, but occasionally strays as far north as Martha's Vineyard, has its skeleton pierced by five elongate, regularly spaced holes. The genus *Mellita* was originally described by the great naturalist, Louis Agassiz.

Living sand dollars are often abundant on sandy bottoms. Their tests are coated with large numbers of velvety fine spines that contrast with the long, sturdy, pointed spines of the closely related purple and green sea urchins. Both the tests and the spines vary from uniform light brown to purplish brown. Sand dollars live just beneath the surface of the sand. When exposed,

Echinodermata • 141

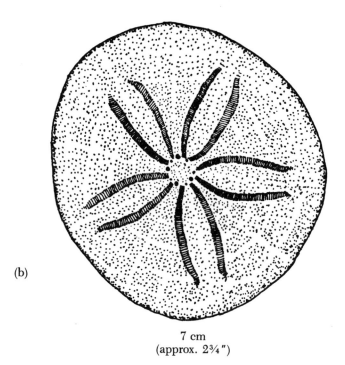

(b)

7 cm
(approx. 2¾")

(b) *Echinarachnius parma*—The Sand Dollar, common from Long Island Sound northward. Upper (aboral) side.

they bury themselves by piling sand in front of them and moving into it. When they die and are washed up on the beach, the spines fall off and the tests eventually bleach and become white. A test from a dead dollar, when we pick it up and shake it, rattles because of the now loosened and dried complicated dentary apparatus, called the Aristotle's Lantern because of its imagined resemblance to an old Greek oil lamp. Aristotle's Lantern in the living animal is an intricate and beautiful structure of five groups of calcareous plates bound by muscles from which five calcium carbonate teeth project to the outside. The teeth are used in capturing the small worms and other organisms on which these animals live.

Sand dollars move by the hydraulic tube-foot system, like the method used by starfish and sea urchins. They manage locomotion by coordinated movements of the spines. In this system, water enters the water-vascular system through minute pores in the sieve plate, goes through canals, and finally enters a hollow contractile bulb at the inner end of each tube foot.

142 • Echinodermata

When the bulb contracts the tube lengthens, and when it is relaxed the tube is withdrawn. The ends of the tube feet are sucking disks. The tube feet coordinate to pull the animal along.

In sand dollars, the sexes are separate; eggs and sperm are spawned directly into the surrounding water through the five small openings around the sieve plate. After fertilization, the larvae develop into free-swimming, planktonic, ciliated, bilaterally symmetrical individuals, and several weeks later they metamorphose into radially symmetrical adults and settle to the bottom. This metamorphosis is one of the most remarkable in the animal kingdom. Only a small percentage survive, for most of the larvae are lost, are eaten, or settle in the wrong environment. The eggs of sand dollars have been a favorite tool of experimental embryologists since the first decades of this century. They are relatively plentiful, hardy, easy to culture in the laboratory, and their habits of growth and development are simple to observe.

Apparently, starfishes are one of the main enemies of sand dollars. When a starfish crosses a bed of sand dollars, the dollars down current from the starfish quickly bury themselves. Flounders, cod, and haddock feed extensively on sand dollars when they can.

Through the ages, the Sand Dollar has been used as both ornament and amulet. In some quarters it is known as the Holy Ghost Shell because the markings on the shell seem to symbolize the birth, crucifixion, and resurrection of Christ. The five-pointed star on the underside of the sand dollar is thought to represent the Star of Bethlehem, and also resembles the outline of an Easter Lily. The narrow elliptical openings are reminiscent of the five wounds made in the body of Christ during crucifixion. On the underside of the shell is an easily recognized outline like that of the Christmas poinsettia. When the shell is broken open, cells are found, each holding five objects that look like five birds in flight. These can represent the doves of peace. Another interpretation of these birdlike objects connects them to the angels who sang to the shepherds on the first Christmas morning.

The Native Sea Cucumbers

Strewn on and buried slightly below the muddy bottoms of shallow embayments bordering the estuaries in the coastal zone of the southern New England states is the rough-coated *Thyone* (or *Sclerodactyla*) *briareus*, member of a rather curious group of animals, the sea cucumbers. These animals belong to the class Holothuroidea, a representative group of the radially symmetrical phylum of pentamerous (divisible into fives), spiny-skinned invertebrates, the Echinodermata.

More widely spread and always found in burrows in firm sand or mud in many subtidal flats is the related genus *Leptosynapta*, often mistaken for a member of one of the groups of worms because of its elongate vermiform (worm-shaped) body. The two species of this animal in our coastal waters are *Leptosynapta inhaerens*, a pale gray creature, and *Leptosynapta roseola*, a roseate beast. We can easily keep the leptosynaptid cucumbers separate from the worms if we notice the five branching tentacles at their anterior ends (almost entirely contractable), the five faint white stripes that run the length of their bodies, and the clinging sensation we get when we run our fingers along the outside of the body. If the tentacles are contracted when you find the animal, put it into a quiet body of seawater until it relaxes and these structures appear.

At first glance, sea cucumbers seem little like such other echinoderms as sea urchins, brittle stars, starfishes, and sea biscuits; nevertheless, they all have the same basic five-part (pentamerous) arrangement. Perhaps the easiest way to see this pattern is to hold the animal vertically and look directly down at it toward the end with the tentacles. Another way to think about sea cucumbers being echinoderms is to view them as disk-shaped starfish that have grown into the shape of a shopping bag pointed at one end and slightly truncated (cut off) at the other.

Holothuroideans use the tentacles for feeding, the mouth being in the center of the crown of tentacles. The tentacles are covered with a fairly sticky mucoid material to which living and nonliving particles adhere. After a tentacle is covered with

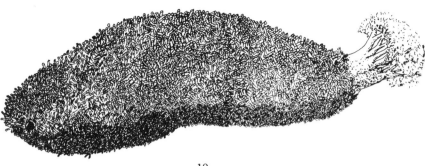

10 cm
(approx. 4")

Thyone briareus—The New England Cucumber.

material it is put into the mouth, and whatever has stuck to it is scraped off. Food consists almost entirely of microscopic fauna and flora, detritus, and one-celled plants, collected as the waving tentacles sweep through the water or along the surface of the sand or mud substratum. Because all three of the local sea cucumbers often live below the surface of the bottom (*Leptosynapta* is characteristically a burrower, and *Thyone* may excavate a U-shaped burrow), they may swallow a great deal of sand, much as an earthworm swallows soil. The material in which they are burrowing is passed through their bodies and the nutritive substances are digested out.

Thus the holothuroideans are the only really successful burrowing forms among the echinoderms, a living habit that has probably been brought about by their armless condition and sausage shape, and because they have a muscular body wall with small, widely separated calcium carbonate skeletal elements. In the other echinoderms, these calcium carbonate ossicles are more numerous and closer together, forming a more or less rigid skeleton.

Although sea cucumbers may be relatively insensitive to light, they have a well-developed sense of touch, which serves them as a means of protection. The worm-shaped leptosynaptids contract sharply, and may break into two or more pieces when mechanically disturbed or roughly handled. The more conventionally shaped globose forms react to this kind of stim-

Echinodermata • 145

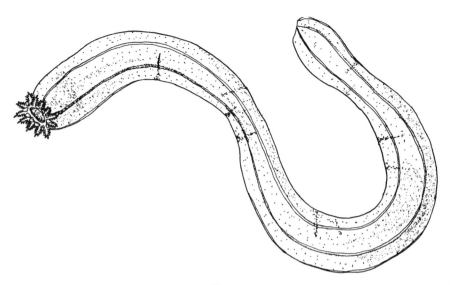

7 cm
(approx. 2¾″)

Leptosynapta inhaerens—The Glass Worm, an elongate, translucent holo-
thurian or sea cucumber.

ulus by contracting the body and rupturing the cloaca, then
expelling the respiratory trees (explained below), the digestive
tract, and the gonads. In *Thyone*, the anterior end ruptures,
expelling the tentacles, pharynx, part of the intestine, and associated organs. This violent reaction is not often fatal, for most
species of holothurians have great powers of regeneration, and
the lost organs are soon replaced. In *Thyone*, the cloacal region
(aboral, the end opposite the tentacles) is the center of regeneration. Great regenerative power in sea cucumbers brings to
mind other echinoderms such as the common Starfish, which
can replace entire lost arms.

Synaptids respire through the general body surface. *Thyone*
and its close relatives, though, have a unique and remarkable
system of tubules, the respiratory trees, one on each side of the
digestive tract. The trunks of the two trees arise from the cloaca, and the pumping action of the cloaca forces water in and
out of the respiratory trees. In this way, new water is constantly
gulped in through the anus and oxygen is brought to various
parts of the body.

146 • Echinodermata

Sea cucumbers ordinarily move around by means of pentamerous (five-ranked) rows of tube feet. The three holothuroideans mentioned above, though, are exceptions. *Thyone* has podia (feet) on both surfaces of the body, with suckers best developed on the podia of the sole; they creep about slowly. *Leptosynapta* lack tube feet altogether and move about using tentacles as holdfasts. These animals push into the sand with alternate contractions of their circular and longitudinal muscles, pushing the sand aside with their tentacles, moving two to three centimeters in an hour. Young leptosynaptids are able to swim by lashing out both ends of the body at the same time while they are temporarily U-shaped.

Reproduction in holothurians is much the same as in other echinoderms, except that even the hermaphroditic members of this class have only one gonad. The eggs of relatives of both *Thyone* and *Leptosynapta* undergo incubation in which the eggs pass through the gonads into the body cavity and are fertilized. Here they are brooded while developing, the young eventually leaving the mother's body by means of a break near the anus and become members of the zooplankton.

Other holothuroideans we may find include the scarlet *Psolus fabricii*; the Orange-footed Cucumber, *Cucumaria frondosa*; the Milky Cucumber, *Chiridota laevis*; and the Rat-tailed Cucumber, *Caudina arenata*.

Although none of the holothurians described above has been used as food, a large warm-water form (*Stichopus*) has a more glutinous and less leathery body wall and is highly prized by the Chinese. The Chinese are said to relish a meal of "trepang," which consists of sun-dried body walls of several species of *Holothuria*, *Stichopus*, and *Thelenota*. "It is employed," says Edward Forbes, "in the preparation of nutritious soups, in common with an esculent seaweed, sharks' fins, edible birds' nests . . . affording much jelly." Holothurians may also come to the table as Bêche-de-Mer.

The Sea Urchin and Its Life

Often found in the tide pools and along some of the rock-strewn shores south from Cape Cod to the West Indies, the Sea Urchin is a curious, slow-moving reddish to dark purplish, hemispherical, spine-covered animal known to the zoologist as *Arbacia punctulata*. It belongs to the same group of organisms as the starfish, sand dollars, and sea lilies, a phylum of radially symmetrical, pentamerous (body divisions and many internal structures occur in fives), ancient beasts, the echinoderms or spiny-skinned animals, found in nearly all the seas on earth.

Arbacia lives along the eastern coast of North America from Woods Hole, Martha's Vineyard, and Nantucket to Florida, often intertidally but more frequently in depths of from 20 to 90 feet and on down to about 700 feet. It more often lives in large, widely separated groups or "beds" of various sized animals rather than as individuals going it alone. The shells or tests of commonly found individuals (measured without the spines) vary from ¼ inch to 2¼ inches in diameter and from ⅛ inch to 1½ inches in height, and are generally about half as high as they are wide. The conical, sharply pointed, but non-poisonous spines, shortest and relatively flat at the base, are longest along the sides, averaging about 1½ inches in this area.

Because the Sea Urchin is radially symmetrical instead of bilaterally symmetrical like ourselves, it has an oral (mouth) and an aboral surface rather than the dorsal and ventral surfaces of vertebrates. The oral surface with its central mouth is the flattened area of the animal, and the aboral surface is punctured at the peak of the dome by a small anus.

Dead sea urchins quickly lose their muscle-attached spines, and when washed up on the beach exhibit a unique pentamerous arrangement of variously punctured and sculptured plates tightly fitted together like the pieces in a newly constructed jigsaw puzzle. The number of plates varies with the size of the individual. The large heart-shaped madreporic plate on the aboral surface is like a sieve through the microscopic holes of which water enters. The water drawn in through this organ is

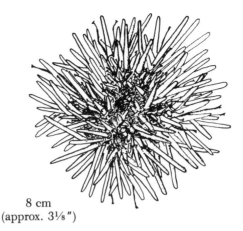

8 cm
(approx. 3⅛ ")

Arbacia punctulata—The Purple Sea Urchin.

vital to the ambulacral (water-walking) system, an organ system found only in echinoderms. Through each of the holes in the lateral plates of the living animal extends a long, slender tube foot, ending with a water-operated suction cup. Above the small, rounded knobs on these plates the spines articulate closely by means of their cup-shaped bases. Between the spines are two- or three-jointed jawlike pedicellaria that wave back and forth, snatching foreign objects from the surface of the Sea Urchin.

When we shake an intact, dried *Arbacia* shell or test, it makes a rattling noise. As in the Sand Dollar, the noise is caused by a rather large and complex dental apparatus called Aristotle's Lantern, because its original description by Aristotle caused later zoologists to mark its resemblance to Greek lanterns of Aristotle's time.

The Sea Urchin may move in any direction, using its spines and tube feet to travel at about one inch per minute. When we put it on its aboral surface in water, *Arbacia* uses these same structures to turn itself over to its normal position. In shallow environments, sea urchins ordinarily move away from the light and are found in shaded or dark areas, often in empty bivalve shells or under overhanging rocks.

To collect *Arbacia*, the best place to look is along rocks or shelly bottoms. The scuba diver can pick them up easily by hand, but from a boat we must drag a "starfish mop" (an

Echinodermata • 149

enlarged version of a kitchen mop) over the bottom. The sea urchins cling to it by their pedicellaria until we bring them on board.

Arbacia can regenerate spines, tube feet, pedicellaria, and, if undisturbed, they can heal shell fractures. They live well in the ordinary saltwater aquarium, and can go without eating for more than a month at a time, apparently without ill effect. They are omnivorous, though, eating a great variety of living material, including Rockweed, Sea Lettuce, coral, sponges, mussels, sand dollars, other *Arbacia*, and live and dead fish.

Great quantities of *Arbacia* have been used since the turn of the century by experimental embryologists in studying phases of growth and development. Much is known, therefore, about the life history of these animals, from the shedding of eggs and sperm, through the planktonic larval stages, to the metamorphosed adult. In spite of the tremendous amount of investigation, zoologists are still unable to tell the sexes apart.

Although sea urchins have been used as human food from time immemorial, it is a larger species, such as the Green Sea Urchin, *Strongylocentrotus drobachiensis*, from the coast of Maine, whose gonads, and particularly the eggs, are highly regarded by gourmets. *Arbacia* is also eaten by many kinds of fish, such as cod and haddock, as well as starfish, spider crabs, and fellow *Arbacia*. Long before the time of Pliny, both raw and cooked sea urchins were used as medicine for many ills, and even as an antidote for some poisonous plants. Not only have the shells or tests been used as cups, flower pots, and even lamps, but they have been found as part of the motif in decorations on ancient vases, coins, and jewelry.

Star of the Sea

The Common Sea Star, or Starfish, as it is often called, lives in the waters of the western Atlantic Ocean from Maine to the Gulf of Mexico, but it is relatively rare north of Massachusetts, where it overlaps the range of the common

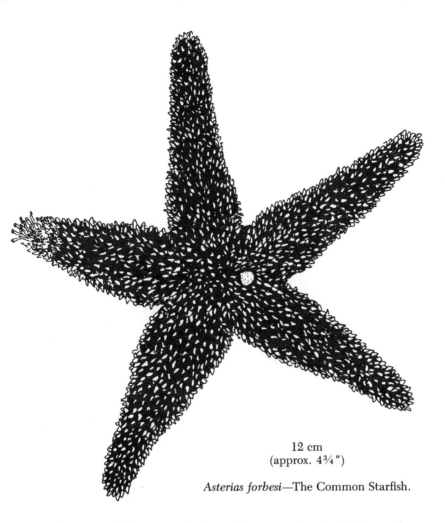

12 cm
(approx. 4¾″)

Asterias forbesi—The Common Starfish.

Northern Starfish or Purple Star, *Asterias vulgaris*. It is mostly a shallow-water form, although it has been found in more than 500 fathoms of water. The best time to beachcomb for it is at low tide, when we may find individuals lurking in the dark corners, crevices, and crannies of tide pools, under or along the sides of rocks and empty shells, or concentrated near collections of live snails or bivalves. Sea stars may be colored from light orange through shades of dark purple or greenish-black. Supposedly, two kinds of sea stars live in mid-New England (Massachusetts and Rhode Island) waters, *Asterias forbesi* (named after the famed Scottish zoologist, Edward Forbes): an animal with stout, blunt cylindrical arms, scattered spines, and a bright orange madreporite (a sieve plate through which water enters the ambulacral system), and *Asterias vulgaris*, with flattened, pointed arms or rays, numerous spines that seem to form an obvious median line on each arm, and a pale yellow madreporite. So many local sea stars have been found intermediate between these two species, though, that a number of zoologists now feel that there is actually only one species.

Sea stars were well known to Aristotle and his contemporaries, and we find interesting and sometimes startling accounts of them in the writings of several medieval naturalists. It was not until 1733, when Johannes Linck, a German zoologist and physician from Leipzig, described their anatomy, that our present knowledge of the group started.

Normally these echinoderms have bodies with the form of a five-rayed star, but some individuals, because of autotomy (ability to cast off a part of the body) and abnormality in subsequent regeneration, may be found with six, seven, eight, or even nine arms. Animals with fewer than five arms, or with arms shorter than others, either have not started to regenerate or have not finished the year necessary to complete new growth.

Like all other echinoderms, sea stars are radially symmetrical, with spicules or plates of calcium carbonate in the body wall forming an internal skeleton, and a system of fluid-carrying tubes and canals extending throughout the body, called a water-vascular or ambulacral system because of its use in locomotion. Sea stars are usually oriented with the surface on which the mouth is located (oral surface) downward or against the substratum. If we turn over a living Sea Star, the membranous area surrounding the mouth (the peristome) is easily seen. From this structure, and extending along the midline of each arm, is a deep grove from which tube feet in four rows wave in all directions. After we put the animal back on its oral surface, we can see at once the general shape of the central disk, with its eccentric and often brilliantly colored circular madreporite and its five radiating arms covered with three types of short spines or tubercles. A hand lens is necessary to see the small anal opening near the center of the disk; the very small jawlike (sometimes extensible) pedicellariae (pincers) distributed over the surface and used to keep this area free of detritus; the miniature fingerlike fleshy growths around the base of the spines with which respiration is accomplished; and the pink to red eye spot at the tip of each arm, surrounded by very small tentacles shaped like common pins. The entire surface of the body is ciliated.

Although the sexes in sea stars are separate, it is nearly impossible to tell the difference between males and females externally except when the latters' arms are plump and relatively soft, filled with large orange eggs. Fertilization of the eggs takes place after the sexual products are shed freely into the salt water. In a short while, they develop into a bilaterally symmetrical larva called a bipinnaria. Breeding season is in the spring; the number of eggs shed depends on the size of the sea star, a nine- to twelve-inch female shedding as many as 2,500,000 eggs. Eventually the bipinnaria larva goes through several additional stages before it undergoes one of the most remarkable changes in the animal kingdom by metamorphosing into a radially symmetrical, easily recognizable Sea Star less than 1 millimeter in diameter, and settles to the bottom.

The size of sea stars depends directly on the amount of food eaten and not on chronological age. Research reveals that in winter the ossicles making up the skeleton shrink together, reducing the overall size of the animals, and that, also at this time of year, the animals migrate in relatively large groups from shallow to deeper waters. Divers and underwater photography reveal that sea stars not only move by means of their tube feet, but that they may be transported passively just above the bottom by tidal currents. These observations explain their unexpected and rapid appearance in large numbers on ground previously unsettled.

The Sea Star is a carnivore, and it is economically important for its highly destructive predation on all the edible mollusks and crustaceans (barnacles) it can reach. The list includes the more familiar commercial species such as oysters, quahogs, mussels, and periwinkles as well as limpets, cockles, and snails and scallops, when they can be caught. Precise statistics for Sea Star predation are not available, but a few examples indicate its power: in 1887, Connecticut estimated that it lost 634,246 bushels of oysters worth $463,000 to these animals; in 1929, one oyster company removed more than 10 million sea stars from 11,000 acres of oyster grounds in Narragansett Bay. A 1961 starfish survey showed that they reached a density of 1,000 to 2,000 for every 2,000 square yards in three regions of Narragansett Bay.

Sea stars are collected from the bay bottom by dredging or by dragging a "starfish mop" over starfish beds. The animals cling to the mops with the pedicellariae and are brought to the decks of the collecting vessels. Before their powers of regeneration were recognized, they were disposed of by tearing them in pieces and tossing them overboard. Today, however, they are more profitably heaped, dried, and ground into fertilizer or included in poultry feed.

It seems strange that in spite of many documented observations over the years, how the Sea Star opens its prey has not been settled to the satisfaction of invertebrate zoologists. Certainly these animals leave no marks on their victims. Apparently, the Sea Star settles on a bivalve with its central disk close to the hinge of its prey, two of its arms spread on one shell and three arranged on the opposite valve. By pulling the shells in opposite directions, with tube feet exerting a force in excess of 6 pounds per square inch, a crack less than $1/32$ inch wide is made, through which narcotizing fluid from the Sea Star's stomach may or may not be injected. But the opening is big enough for the Sea Star to insert its everted stomach. The soft parts of the live mollusk are quickly digested, the stomach is drawn back inside the predator's body from the now empty shells of its prey, and the Sea Star moves on in search of its next victim.

Among other starfish that we may find is the smaller bright red (sometimes orange, yellowish, or purple) Blood Star, *Henricia* spp., a bottom dweller in colder offshore waters. This star, having only two rows of tube feet, feeds on sponges rather than on mollusks, and carries its young in a brood pouch instead of releasing fertilized eggs into the water. North of Cape Cod, the large Gold Bordered Sea Star, *Hippasteria phrygiana*, is washed up on occasion. It is a striking animal, its body covered with tiny bivalved clam-shaped pedicellariae, and is red with a golden border and with distinct upper and lower marginal plates.

Mollusca

One of the Most Primitive Living Marine Mollusks

A long the rocky groins of the harbors, and among the tide pools formed by cobbles and boulders, live biologically interesting members of the most primitive class of mollusks that inhabit these shallow waters. These animals, commonly known as chitons (from the Greek word for tunic or coat of mail), are nearly worldwide in distribution, belong to the class Amphineura, and to the order Polyplacophora. *Chaetopleura apiculata*, common along the entire East Coast from Cape Cod to Florida, is considered to be the most successful of the molluscan minor groups.

Similar to its close relatives, *Tonicella marmorea* and *Ischnochiton ruber*, which range in deep waters from Long Island Sound northward and become circumpolar, the more southerly *Chaetopleura* are greatly flattened mollusks, with a rudimentary head that differs from the heads of most snails (Gastropoda) in having neither tentacles nor eyes. The feature that readily distinguishes chitons from other mollusks is the shell of eight slightly overlapping plates or valves arranged in a longitudinal row covering the dorsal (top) surface of the animal. This shell, secreted by the underlying mantle, is surrounded by a girdle (part of the mantle), whose ornamentation is readily revealed by the microscope. The sculpturing of the shell is practical for the Chiton because most often it is caused by very small canals associated with sense organs called aesthetes.

In *Chaetopleura*, the girdle surrounding the plates is hairy, and the plates are gray or yellowish, sometimes with a reddish tinge. An obvious keel runs along the center of each of the plates, and the plates in turn are covered irregularly with small tubercles.

The ventral (bottom) surface of chitons is nearly all foot; it is typically broad and flat, and is used to adhere to shells or to a

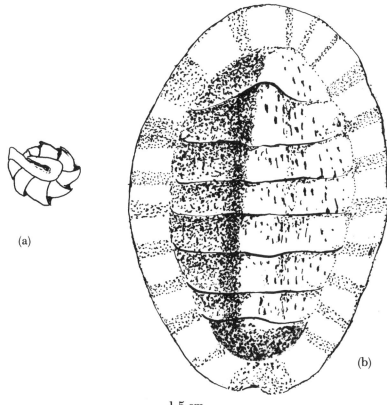

(a)

(b)

1.5 cm
(approx. ⅝")

Chaetopleura apiculata—The Common Eastern Chiton. (a) When disturbed, the chiton curls up like a pill bug. (b) Clearly shows the dorsal armature of 8 transverse calcareous plates.

rocky substratum. Propulsion is accomplished entirely by muscular waves along the sole of the foot. When we strenuously attempt to detach these animals, the girdle is forcibly applied against the rock and the foot is retracted. This reaction enables the ventral surface to form a powerful suction cup, and makes removal of the animal quite difficult. For this reason, chitons usually are found on smooth rocks and shells because of the better adhesion provided by a smooth surface. If we are lucky enough to loosen its hold, it rolls into a ball much like a pill bug or a sow bug when we pick it up, the dorsal valves forming a protective covering or shield.

Mollusca • 157

Spawning in chitons usually shows some lunar periodicity. Although the sexes are separate, it is almost impossible to differentiate visually the males from the females. The females do not shed their ova until the males have released their sperm into the surrounding water, but exactly what causes the male to start doing so is not known. One hypothesis for the start of male sperm release holds that this reaction is a response to a chemical stimulus from the female. Fortunately, chitons are generally gregarious, because grouping enables at least some sperm to reach the females and fertilize the ova inside the mantle cavity. The eggs are shed into the sea in masses or strings. Fertilized eggs soon develop into a planktonic (floating) larva that metamorphoses directly into a bottom-living juvenile, a small edition of its parents.

Most of the 600 known species of chitons are inconspicuously colored, their dull shades of red, brown, yellow, or green blending into their rock-strewn background and providing excellent protection from their enemies. Nearly all Atlantic Coast chitons are less than three inches long. *Chaetopleura* is drab in color and grows to a length of about ¾ inch. The largest forms have been collected on the Pacific Coast, *Katherinia* and *Ischnochiton* reaching a length of about twelve inches. Although these animals have been found to a depth of 12,000 feet, *Chaetopleura*, like most other chitons worldwide, lives in shallow, barely subtidal waters in areas where the bottom is lined with rocks and sometimes shells.

Unlike many other mollusks, chitons wander very little unless they are disturbed. If we turn over a rock bearing a Chiton, the animal will slowly make its way to the underside of the rock, a good example of photonegativity. They ordinarily stay in a closely circumscribed area, feeding on algae and other material scraped from the rocky substratum with their seven jaws and their unusually long radula; this toothed structure scrapes small particles from the rocks with a rhythmic back-and-forth motion. The radula is a ribbonlike structure bearing many transverse rows of teeth, with seventeen teeth in a row, the central teeth being largest. It has been observed that when a subradular organ, apparently sensory or a chemoreceptor, is applied against the substratum, the subradular organ is immediately retracted and replaced by the radula after food is located. On occasion, individuals may go on a short scouting trip, returning to the precise spot they started from, after satisfying their appetites. Some chitons are so adapted to one location that their girdle becomes shaped to the irregularities of the substratum, but other species find and then live permanently in cavities or depressions in the rock surfaces that provide their bodies with a fairly close fit.

Most of the feeding activities occur at night, for it is then that the chitons come out from the dark places inhabited during the day. Chiton collecting is most successful out on the rocks or in tide pools on foggy or cloudy days. When the sun is out, we must find them by turning over loose rocks at low tide.

The American Indians of the Pacific Northwest and the natives of the West Indies discovered independently the virtues and pleasures of dining on the local large species of chitons. They later became one of the favorite foods of the Russians who first settled Alaska. The chitons of our coast are too small and too difficult to collect enough of to make them a common dish in this part of the country.

Chitons may be removed from a rock with a sudden well-directed, sideways blow before the animal can pull itself tightly to the substratum, or, failing this tactic, by inserting a thin knife blade between rock and the animal's muscular foot. The edible part of the Chiton is the flesh foot, and according to those who have tried it, it is delicious raw, with or without lemon juice or cocktail sauce. In the West Indies, Chiton meat is known as "sea beef." It may be fried or boiled, and is used in soups and chowders.

Jingle Shells, the Beachcomber's Delight

The very handsome, slightly convex oval shells with a yellow or golden mother-of-pearl sheen, often found high on exposed marine beaches, are the so-called Jingle Shells, also known as Mermaid's Toenails, from their general shape. The outer surface of living jingles is scaly and dark colored,

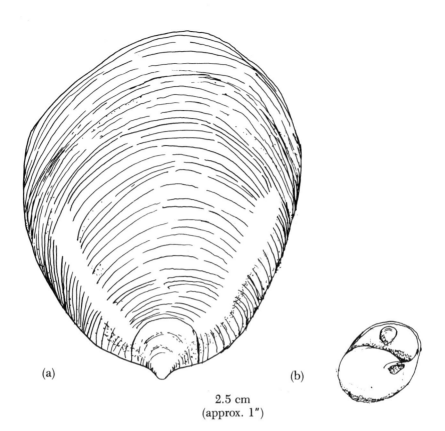

(a)

(b)

2.5 cm
(approx. 1")

Crepidula plana—The Flat Slipper Shell. (a) External view; notice the minute apex. (b) Customary position, adhering to interior of moon shell inhabited by a hermit crab.

sometimes covered with groups of prickly radiating lines. When the animals die, this rough covering is usually worn off, exposing the silvery or translucent shades beneath.

The two species of jingle shells in these waters are the small *Anomia aculeata*, whose irregularly rounded and moderately fragile shell is no more than about 25 millimeters (about an inch) in diameter, and the more common and larger *Anomia simplex*, an animal with a thin but strong shell, ordinarily twice the size of *Anomia aculeata*. Both mollusks have been known for a long time, the larger of the two having appeared in the tenth edition of *Systema Naturae* (1758), by Carolus Linnaeus. Though *Anomia aculeata* ranges from Long Island to the Arctic Ocean, it is most common attached to rocks and

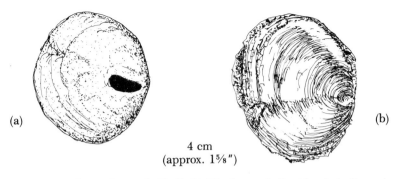

(a)

(b)

4 cm
(approx. 1⅝ ")

Anomia simplex—The Jingle Shell. (a) Flat lower shell with a hole through which the byssal threads attach the animal to rocks or other shells. (b) The upper valve of the shell.

broken shells in waters north of Cape Cod from one to eighty fathoms down. It is also found in Europe. *Anomia simplex* has been collected from Nova Scotia, southward around the Florida peninsula, to Texas; and it occurs in the West Indies and in Europe. In all these areas, it lives in shallow sublittoral waters and is especially abundant on oyster beds, logs, wharves, and sometimes even on boats. Individuals buried in mud are blackened, but we can restore normal coloration by exposing them to free-flowing sea water. Although the Jingle is eaten in Europe, we in this country apparently have not yet discovered how delicious this bivalve really is.

The jingle shells belong in the family *Anomiidae*, one of about a dozen families of the order *Filibranchia* that include such more or less commonly found shellfish as oysters, scallops, pearl oysters, Kitten Paws, mussels, and the ark shells or cockles. The generic name, *Anomia*, is derived from the Greek "anomos," meaning irregular or uneven, and undoubtedly refers to the uneven sizes or asymmetry of the two shells. The upper or free valve is usually quite convex, whereas the much smaller lower valve is flat and has a hole near its apex or hinge end. The lower shell is molded, and cemented so firmly to whatever it is fastened to that it never breaks free—only the top shells of the animals are washed ashore whenever the substratum of living or dead jingles is disturbed enough to cause the shells to part company.

Unlike the Oyster, the Jingle fastens itself to rocks or other substrata by its right or lower valve. It is through the nearly

Mollusca • 161

circular hole or deep embayment in this flat shell that the calcified band of byssus is extended to fix the animal to a resting place for the remainder of its life. If you recall, the byssus is a special gland in the foot of filibranchians that secretes tough, viscous threads that are first attached when the foot is extended and pressed against the substratum. Then, as this organ retracts from the bottom, the threads are spun out and coalesce into a cable that hardens and calcifies on contact with water. Byssal retractor muscles are attached from the bottom to the upper shell and, like the shell muscles of the Limpet, pull the animal down against the substratum. This animal (like the Limpet) therefore has really only one functional valve, the movable upper shell, the edge of which clamps down close against the hard bottom.

Jingle shells lack siphons, a characteristic they share with scallops, but not with clams. Like all other bivalves, though, they have ciliated gills. The cilia are spread along the gill surface, and are used to build a food-collecting and a food-storing device. This mechanism draws small particles and microscopic organisms over the gill surfaces, where they are delivered and concentrated in ciliated food grooves. The food grooves carry this material to the small, flaplike palps (fleshy sensory projections). Here the food is sorted, and the items of acceptable size are conveyed to the mouth, where they are ingested.

Both *Anomia simplex* and *Anomia aculeata* have been found in biologically interesting associations with other organisms. The species are most often observed living in the same habitat, the larger one attached to oysters more than to any other organisms. Some years ago, a marine invertebrate zoologist at the Marine Biological Laboratory in Woods Hole was working on a marine polychaete, *Polydora*, a relative of the Clam Worm, which lives in shells of bay scallops, *Argopecten* (formerly *Aequipecten*) *irradians*. He found that the population of scallops with *Anomia simplex* attached by its calcified byssus threads had far fewer *Polydora* than clean scallops, or scallops with other attached organisms. He judged that the presence of *Anomia* on scallop shells exerted more or less exclusive influence in keeping *Polydora* away from scallops.

Children prefer jingle shells to many other kinds of shells easily collected on our beaches; jingles are usually plentiful, they are bright and pretty, they are easily used in handicrafts, and they rarely need to be cleaned or polished.

> *We collect the jingle shell so numerous*
> *By means of ulna, radius, and humerus,*
> *And bring them to the creative dreamers*
> *On tired tibias and fibulas and femurs!*

It Reminded the Greeks of a Mouse

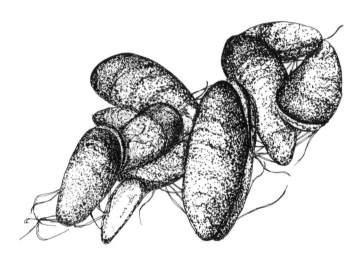

15 cm
(approx. 6")

Mytilus edulis—The Sea or Edible Mussel often lives in the most heavily populated part of the intertidal region, among the plants low on a rocky shore, with a large variety of both sessile and mobile invertebrates.

*O*n this part of the Atlantic Coast, the opportunity to become a gourmet at little expense and effort is tremendous. The salt waters here harbor a great number of marine organisms that could and should be included in our diet.

One delicacy that the French discovered long ago is the Edible Mussel—a smooth-shelled blue to violet to blue-black, three- to six-inch mollusk whose scientific name is *Mytilus edulis*. The mussel has a sweet, nutlike flavor that will appeal to those who object to the "fishy" taste of some shellfish.

Mussels grow in clusters of up to 500 on both exposed and unexposed areas of bays, ponds, inlets, and rocky outcrops. Each sea or edible mussel is anchored by a "byssus" or beard to a stone, rock piling, or similar substratum.

It is possible to confuse the edible Sea Mussel with species of horse mussels, which are not nearly as palatable, but which it resembles closely. Three differences between sea mussels and horse mussels (*Modiolus modiolus*) help us tell them apart easily: (1) the Sea Mussel is smooth and blue-black, but the dark brown Horse Mussel is ribbed with long ridges; (2) the Sea Mussel is nearly always found growing in clusters, but horse mussels grow as individuals half-buried in intertidal mud flats, cord grass flats, or mud banks; and (3) the beak (raised part or pointed end) is at the extreme end of the shell of the Sea Mussel, but in the Horse Mussel it is farther back.

The Greeks get credit for the name of the mussel, which is derived from their word meaning mouse. The best guess is that the Greeks had in mind the dark shell of the mussel, which we can suppose resembles the coat of a sleeping mouse.

Oysters "R" for Eating

Let us royster with the oyster—in the shorter days and
*   moister,*
They are brought by brown September, with its roguish final
*   "R";*
For breakfast or for supper, on the under shell or upper,
Of dishes he's the daisy, and of shell-fish he's the star.
                              —*Detroit Free Press*, October 12, 1889

Probably no animal—certainly no other mollusk—has had so much written about it, all in a pleasurable vein, for the past two thousand years. It has been praised by gourmet and by gourmand, adulated by poet and playwright, and has in-

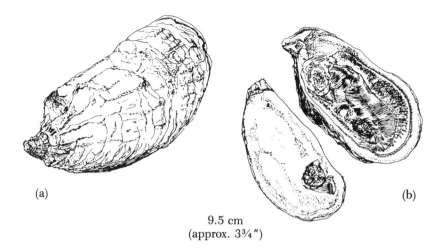

(a)

(b)

9.5 cm
(approx. 3¾″)

Crassostrea virginica—The American Oyster. (a) Outside of the deeper left valve. (b) Left and right valves. The body of the oyster is seen in its normal position in the left valve.

spired the brushes of such artists as Van der Meer, Steen, and Manet. Oysters have titillated the human palates wherever and whenever eating became an art instead of a necessity.

For its gustatory qualities, if for no others, the Oyster has attracted the attention of zoologists who have sought methods of helping it grow and maintain itself in the face of the ever-increasing pressures of the marketplace.

Oysters are sessile organisms, and structurally are extensively adapted to this sedentary way of life. A minute larval stage becomes a part of the great body of marine zooplankton (the microscopic organisms that wander about at the mercy of wind, current, and wave), until it settles on some hard object such as a rock or a shell fragment on the bottom. This small creature, now metamorphosed into a recognizable though minute bivalve, is cemented to the substratum by its right valve or shell. During this change, the foot disappears and the gill extends around the entire rounded part of the animal between the shells. If the Oyster has settled in a favorable environment, it will reach commercial size, from three to four inches long, in from three to five years. Six-inch specimens are not uncommon, and twelve- to fifteen-inch oysters have been found in waters off the New York and New England coasts. The Oyster is just about the only bivalve mollusk with unlike shells, and its shape depends on that of the object to which it is attached. The very large, more or less convex oysters sold in restaurants, are known as "saddlebacks." On a menu, oysters usually are named for the place from which they came; thus "Cotuits" come from the south shore of Cape Cod, "Blue Points" from Long Island Sound, and so on.

According to Paul Galtsoff, dean of American investigators on the biology of oysters, the environment itself may interfere with the welfare of oyster populations. Negative factors in the environment may decrease or inhibit reproductive capabilities, destroy the population by causing extremely adverse conditions, such as increasing incidence of disease, slowing the animal's growth, and at the same time interfering with the development of its main means of defense, the shell. On the positive side, the primary factors that favor health, propagation, and growth of the oyster bed, as the oyster community is called, are the character of the bottom, natural movements of water, salinity of the water, water temperature, and abundance of proper food.

Oysters grow equally well on a hard, rocky, or shell-strewn bottom, on mud compact enough to support their weight, and on a great variety of artificial underwater structures. They apparently thrive best where water is freely exchanged; an ideal nonturbulent flow of water over the oyster bed will carry away excreted material and feces, and at the same time provide oxygen and planktonic food. No *Crassostrea virginica* can survive several hours' exposure to below-freezing temperatures, and so it does not grow near the surface in latitudes (such as ours) where in winter it may be killed at low tide, or frozen in ice and carried away by tidal currents. Oysters are euryhaline organisms, which means that they are able to live in seawater that ranges widely in salt content. When these animals live in parts of estuarine areas in which the salinity gets below ten parts per thousand, though, they may be harmed by fresh water; Victor Loosanoff has shown experimentally that the reproductive capability of oysters can be drastically inhibited by such dilution. Unlike many other species of oysters, *Crassostrea virginica* can live in waters that range from 1° to about 36° Celsius (up to 97°F), but oysters living intertidally or on shallow sand flats exposed to longer than several hours of more extreme temperatures usually die. Being headless, oysters feed by filtering the water as it passes over the gills, retaining and passing toward their mouths selected microorganisms that become embedded in the mucus secreted and discharged by special cells. These cells are part of the ciliated tissue that covers the gills. The best environment for *Crassotrea* to feed in apparently is pollution-free water containing a low concentration of small phytoplankters (diatoms and dinoflagellates) passing across these oysters at a reasonable speed in a nonturbulent flow.

Unique among bivalves is the Oyster's sex life. A large Oyster may spawn as many as 60,000,000 eggs at a time; however, averaging edible oysters of all sizes, a conservative figure would be nearer 25,000,000. Their sexual eccentricities are more interesting. The American Oyster starts essentially as a hermaphrodite, as a male, as a female, or undifferentiated, and changes its sex repeatedly. In the colder waters of New England, many oysters ordinarily change sex once a year during the warmer months; during the winter months, they become neutral or inactive. The zoologist calls this type of behavior alternative sexuality.

What happened in Rhode Island is a very good example of what has occurred to the oyster harvest in virtually all of the oyster-producing states in the Union during the past 30 years. At one time, in the early Fifties and before, really not so very long ago, the oyster harvest in Rhode Island waters was valued at hundreds of thousands of dollars. According to the *Historical Fishery Statistics*, published by the National Marine Fisheries Service, in 1961, only 8800 pounds of oysters (oyster meats) were marketed, bringing in $8259. In 1970, the commercial catch in Rhode Island went down to 7000 pounds valued at $9000; in 1972, it was 3000 pounds worth $5,000; and in 1984, the records show a catch of 1917 pounds valued wholesale at $8845. The decline of the oyster fishery in Rhode Island and elsewhere has been shown to be caused largely by disregard for the cleanliness and general housekeeping in our coastal waters. With stringent measures for pollution control and abatement from all man-created sources, and with concerned management, the disappearing oyster can once more become a plentiful and affordable asset to both the commercial fisherman and our dinner table.

The verse from the *Detroit Free Press* prefacing this article illustrates a belief held until recently that oysters should be eaten only during the months of the year with an "R" in their names, which occur during summer. The idea behind this belief was fairly sound, for temperature affects the life of the oyster by controlling the rate of water transport and hence the feeding, respiration, formation of gonads, and spawning of these animals. The period of maximal feeding and growth in *Crassostrea* is during the colder winter months, and the reproductive season is restricted to the summer months. Oysters then are less fat and least desirable for eating, fullest of reproductive products for continued replacement, and spoil quickest when removed from their environment during the R-less summer months. Today, though, with rapid transportation and modern refrigeration, spoilage and loss have been decreased until it is safe to eat oysters in this part of the world the year around—although gourmets agree without exception that they are not nearly as delicious as those collected during the cool seasons.

The Sharpest Clam

As we walk along the coastal beaches of the Atlantic at low tide on a beautiful summer day, treading the damp and sometimes compacted sand between the tidelines, it is difficult to realize that this apparently barren section of the intertidal beach is probably home to an unbelievably large number of sizable animals. The bivalves, snails, worms, and crustaceans are buried beneath the surface with scarcely a trace visible except to the practiced observer.

The mostly ill-defined tracks and trails will help find some of these animals, but for the many beasts that do not leave their burrows, we must be able to identify the makers by holes, tubes, and channels that we can detect. The shapes and sizes of the excavated sediment associated with the holes are unique for

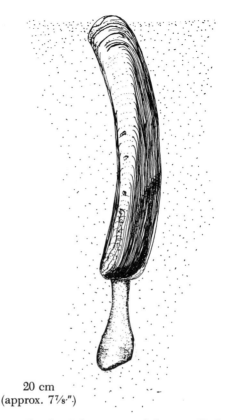

20 cm
(approx. 7⅞".)

Ensis directus—The Razor Clam. The clam's foot is extended as it pulls the animal into the sand beach.

most species, and the types and styles of the sometimes elaborately constructed tubes are characteristic for many forms. The most profitable method is to study the hole or the tube, perhaps photograph it, and then excavate the animal.

Unfortunately, with only a little experience we will not find it easy to dig out a burrowing animal from an intertidal sand flat. The difficulty is not with those near the surface, but with the ones which either live in long tubes deep in the substratum, or which can dig almost as fast as we can shovel. One of the latter group, and probably the fastest bivalve digger on our beaches, is the common or Northern Razor Clam, sometimes called the Northern Jackknife Clam, *Ensis directus*, an animal that uses its lone muscular foot for digging. Its hole on the sand surface is small, elongated, more or less oval, with slightly

Mollusca • 169

sloping sides near the entrance, and with no sand or castings piled around it. If the first or second shovelful does not expose the clam, try another spot, for the animal may be somewhere in the wet sand that is pouring back into the original excavation.

The adult Razor Clam, from four to ten inches long and up to about 1¼ inches wide, depends on its burrowing speed for protection from the turmoil of washing waves. These animals can bury themselves completely in less than seven seconds.

According to the well-known English marine invertebrate authority, C. M. Yonge, "When the tide is in, the animals approach near enough to the surface for the short siphons to project above this, but when the water leaves the sand they retreat deeper, although their presence may be indicated by shallow depressions from which sudden jets of water and sand may be forced up by the animal. To be caught, they must be approached with caution, because razor-shells are highly sensitive to vibrations and at once retreat still deeper. A sudden dig with a spade or a tined fork may bring up an intact specimen, more often a broken portion. . . . A less exhausting mode of capture is to place a handful of table salt over the hole; as this dissolves, the increased salinity irritates the animal below and it may come to the surface and project the hinder end of the shell sufficiently for it to be seized and, with a sudden jerk, pulled out intact. Any hesitation will give the foot time to get a grip on the sand below and it may succeed in pulling the shell down, or else the animal may be literally torn in two between the opposing pull of hand above and foot below."

The clam can put up such a fight because the thick, flattened, rectangular, arrow-shaped foot can be projected half the length of the shell, its tip expanded by being made turgid with blood to form a bulbous anchor in the sand, and its strong muscle rapidly contracted to pull the clam downward. If we carefully place the captured clam horizontally in the water, it will often leap forward by a kind of water-jet propulsion.

The common Razor Clam received its name because it resembles nothing so much as the handle of an old-fashioned straight razor. The sharp-edged, mostly white shells of living healthy specimens are most often covered by a relatively bright greenish-yellow thin layer (*periostracum*) with a long purplish area near the curving edge. Older razor clams and dead Razor Clam shells retain this coloration only in part, and will bear the scars of abrasion as well as the appearance of abraded growth rings toward the more rounded end.

The internal anatomy and life history of the common Razor Clam differ little from those of other common lamellibranch pelecypods (bivalves) such as the Steamer Clam, Quahog, Cockle, and Wood Borer, except for adaptations to a way of living that we have seen. The posterior half is elongated, the *umbones* (original or earliest parts of the shell) are at the extreme anterior end. From this same end protrude the short siphons. They are united for about half their length. The dorsal side of the shell bearing the long external ligament is concave, and the ventral side convex. The ventral edges of the *mantle* (organ that encloses the bivalve viscera and secretes the shell) are entirely fused except for a small opening that lies posteriorly near the base of the siphons. Its anatomical adaptations, of course, seem closely connected with its unique habits. *Ensis directus* has been found in intertidal and subtidal sands from Labrador to the west coast of Florida.

A closely related animal, the Fragile Razor Clam or the Atlantic Razor Clam, *Siliqua costata*, about as common as *Ensis* in our shallow-water sand flats, but not as noticeable, perhaps because it is smaller (two inches long by about ¾ inch wide), has a more restricted range, being found from Nova Scotia to Cape Hatteras. It has a thin, shining, elliptical, fragile shell that more often than not is covered by an iridescent periostracum that may lean to green or to purple. A white, fairly thick raised rib, which extends from the umbo across the inner surface of each shell to the lower margin, often remains as a fragment on the beach, after the rest of the shell has been destroyed. This animal does not have the remarkable burrowing habits of *Ensis*.

In my opinion, *Ensis* is one of our tastiest mollusks. It is excellent in chowder, and fried; it easily tops the steamer clam, *Mya arenaria*. In fact, razor clams may be prepared for the table in nearly as many ways as the common soft-shell and hard-shell clams. If you are one of those happily adventurous souls who wish to extend their gustatory pleasure, I recommend highly and without reservation the Razor Clam.

Termites of the Sea

Wooden timbers and pilings riddled with contiguous holes are a common sight on older docks and wharves or washed up on beaches. Because of the neatness and detail with which they have been made, these holes seem to have been bored by an experienced craftsman. The artisan is the so-called Shipworm, *Teredo navalis*, a highly specialized bivalve (mollusk) especially adapted for boring into wood. Shipworms are most closely related to the Piddocks, animals known to shell collectors as Wing Shells or Angel Wings because of their snowy-white, winglike valves (shells).

The valves of shipworms are two anterior vestigial (remnant) shells, about half an inch long and shaped like a double rasping organ, and two tiny leaflike or paddle-shaped pallets at the base of the siphons (two tubes providing for the intake and exit of water) that protect them from damage. The outer surface of each valve is sculptured with fine ridges, with two rows of file-like teeth with which the Shipworm scrapes the wood. The repeated, alternating rhythmic contraction and relaxation of special muscles at eight to twelve times a minute enables the animal to rasp off fine particles of wood. Although the wood fragments pass through its digestive tract, the Shipworm apparently does not digest all the cellulose of the wood cuttings and convert it to sugar. The remainder is ejected, unchanged in composition, through the excurrent siphon.

The larger part of the animal's body is soft, lies outside the shell, and may be twelve inches and more in length in a full-grown adult. It occupies the tunnel that it has excavated, and has at the same time lined with calcareous or shell-like material.

Like many other sessile marine invertebrates, the minute larvae of shipworms are motile and live for about three weeks as members of the zooplankton. At this time, if the larva is sufficiently fortunate to settle on a submerged timber, it bores a minute hole just large enough to permit entrance of its body. This excavation is only the beginning; it continues to bore, enlarging the hole as its body grows in length and diameter.

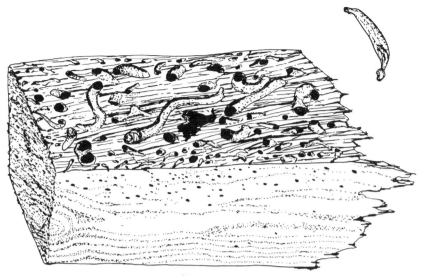

3.7 cm
(approx. 1½")

Teredo navalis—The Shipworm. A wormlike bivalve mollusk that does tremendous damage to chemically untreated wood docks and ships by burrowing long tunnels in the supporting timbers.

Communication to the outside is maintained by a delicate pair of siphons, one pumping in sea water replete with oxygen and microscopic food, and the other pumping out the body wastes. The rate of boring is faster in young animals; a three-month-old individual bores about three-quarters of an inch a day.

Because the Teredo, the commonest local Shipworm, never enlarges the entrance, it must remain in its burrow for life. It does continue to tunnel with the grain of the wood, following the course of least resistance, turning aside for knots or the burrows of neighboring shipworms. Because the entrance holes are minute, the damage produced by boring shipworms often goes undetected until the interior of the timber is completely destroyed, and eventually the wood becomes so weakened by riddling teredos that it falls apart.

Sexual reproduction in the Teredo is protandrous (all are males first), and W. R. Coe, who studied their life history, states that "there is a graded series of ambisexual or hermaphroditic individuals." Ruth L. Turner pointed out that in the young there are two types of males, those which soon change to females, and those which remain males for nearly the entire life of the animal. Fertilization in the Atlantic shipworms occurs after the sperm, shed into the sea water, are taken into the female through the incurrent siphon, where they contact the small white eggs.

Because of their destructiveness to wharves, pilings, ships' hulls, and wooden lobster traps, shipworms are often referred to as termites of the sea. Although they decimate much marine construction and are thus economically important, they are useful in the continuing cycle of sea elements because they help reduce the wood mechanically to its constituent parts. Interestingly, Shipworms are eaten as delicacies by Australian aborigines.

The Shipworm has been known and dreaded since classical times; it is recorded as having riddled the planking of Greek triremes and Roman galleys. Later on, it is known to have destroyed Sir Francis Drake's *Golden Hind*, and in the eighteenth century, it threatened the dykes of Holland. Between 1914 and 1920, in San Francisco Bay, it caused damage estimated at $10 million to ferries, pilings, and warehouses. The longevity of a piling may be much increased by creosoting. Copper sheathing works well for boats, but is impracticable for protecting pilings. During World War II, the study of marine boring mollusks benefited from a research program of the U.S. Navy that resulted in antifouling paints and other materials that have provided increasing protection from these destructive animals.

As so often happens in cases of this kind, there are side effects in the use of these materials. These include most importantly an ever-increasing concentration of metals contained in the anti-fouling paints in and on the bottoms of boat harbors and marinas. These pollutants are washed out slowly over time from the bottoms of boats of all kinds. Unfortunately, this kind of pollution adversely affects the living organisms such as mollusks, worms, tunicates, etc., living in and on the substrata of such facilities.

The Surf Clam: The Atlantic Coast's Largest Marine Bivalve

*I*n homes and offices of beach strollers who have regularly beachcombed the strands fronting the more exposed and sand-flattened, low, sloping beaches, one often sees shells of the large and nearly triangular "Surf Clam," also called "Hen Clam" or "Skimmer." The largest marine bivalve along this coast and often the most common clam shell on ocean beaches south of Cape Cod, *Spisula solidissima*, because of its size and shape, provides shells that serve well for ashtrays, or as parts of handcrafted shell ornaments or beach montages.

Spisula occurs from Labrador to Cape Hatteras, North Carolina, and may grow to more than seven inches long by four and one-half inches wide. The inside of the shell is yellowish-white—dead-white after being repeatedly washed by tidal waters and bleached in the sun, and a large central beak covers a moderate-sized spoon-shaped cavity. In this cavity is a dark brown, elastic, cartilaginous mass that helps the shells to spring open when the muscles release.

As might be expected with a shell of these dimensions, this internal hinge, just below the membranes, is unusually strong. In living animals, the outside of the shell is either smooth or covered with concentric growth lines.

As the name implies, the Surf Clam usually lives just seaward of the mean low-water mark, where it travels just below the surface of the sand. (More live surf clams are usually found washed up on winter than on summer beaches, though, because of the more frequent storms that stir individuals from depths as great as a hundred feet.) Here it burrows ahead with its strong, ivory-colored, tongue-shaped or hatchetlike foot. A unique method of collecting these animals has been developed: a wooden building lath is sharpened on one end, and then at high tide it is dragged and plunged into the bottom. If the sharpened end of the stick passes between the opened shells of a Surf Clam, the animal snaps together tightly, fastening onto the stick and making it possible to pull the clam to the surface.

16 cm
(approx. 6¼ ")

Spisula solidissima—The Surf or Hen Clam.

In general, clams and quahogs are relatively defenseless creatures that rely on hiding in the substratum for protection. The main enemies of this clam apparently are whelks and starfish. When one of these predators barely touches a Surf Clam, the latter is able almost to leap out of the way by rapidly manipulating its foot. It extends the flexible, muscular foot between its shells, anchoring it in the sand and pulling the rest along after it. Herring gulls also enjoy surf clams, and in some areas the clams must be an important article in their diet, if we judge by the large number of cracked *Spisula* shells scattered on hard-surfaced roads and rocks throughout the length and breadth of the clam's distribution. The gull picks up the clam in its claws, and flies skyward about a hundred feet, drops the clam, and then swoops down to pick and swallow greedily the soft parts of the cracked mollusk.

Spisula is a fairly close relative of both *Mercenaria mercenaria*, the Common Quahog, and the larger offshore *Arctica islandica*, the Black Quahog, whose large populations and great economic potential were discovered in the early 1940s by Charles J. Fish, first director of the Narragansett Marine Laboratory. Like these other two bivalves, the Surf Clam has an open circulatory system with a heart that should be excellent for physiological study: it is easy to reach, and can be readily perfused with solutions whose effects on the rate of heartbeat can be observed and recorded. Embryologists too are interested in *Spisula* because it has mature eggs and sperm late in the summer, after most other local bivalves have finished spawning. At this time, the uniquely colored, pinkish eggs and white sperm may be obtained easily from the ovaries and the testes, respectively, of mature animals.

One reason that marine invertebrate ecologists have worked with *Spisula* has to do with its feeding habits. In this animal, which feeds just above the surface of the bottom on material suspended in the surrounding water, the siphons are unusually short, and their openings are strongly fringed. It has been observed that the tentacles around the incurrent siphon, the tube-shaped organ that carries water with its microscopic food particles into the body of the clam, are an efficient filtering mechanism, keeping out materials unsuitable for the digestive system.

By local custom in some uninformed areas, people use surf clams only as fish bait, but it is easy to convert these animals into one of the most luscious shellfish delicacies obtainable for the taking. After finding a good surf clam bed (usually sandpits and sandbars just submerged at mid-tide), we wait until the low tide that occurs a day or so after a full or new moon, and then search and harvest the bed by hand.

If you include surf clams in clambakes, use only the young, smaller specimens. Euell Gibbons, author of *Stalking the Blue-Eyed Scallop*, advocates opening the clams with a thin, round-ended knife, draining the bluish clam juice into a kettle to be drunk from a cup as clam "chocter" (nectar plus chowder) made by heating it with an equal quantity of milk and seasoning with freshly ground black pepper. He then removes the abductor muscles, which he calls "beach scallops," rinses them in clam juice, and recommends eating them raw as they are, or chilled with either cocktail sauce or melted-butter. They may be fried or made into a delicious clam chowder, and they freeze well when placed in a container and covered with clam juice.

Queen Quahog

*P*robably one of the two best known bivalves along the shallow, protected salt waters on southern New England is the bivalve or pelecypod, *Mercenaria mercenaria*, more commonly known as the Quahog; Quahog being the white man's attempt to pronounce the Indian name for this animal. Although it is found in sheltered bays and coves the length of the Atlantic Coast from the Gulf of St. Lawrence to the Texas seaboard on the Gulf of Mexico, it is most abundant from Cape Cod southward.

The scientific name of this animal, unlike those of many of its relatives, is reflected in the uses to which it has been put by people: *Mercenaria* is derived from the Latin word for "wages." It is thought that the taxonomist Carl Linnaeus, in giving the pelecypod this name, took into consideration that American Indians living along the coast ground the shells of this animal into cylindrical beads, from which they made "wampum" or Indian money. For this purpose, the often-prominent purple area along the ventral margin inside the shells and near the muscle scars was particularly valuable, worth more than twice as much as the ordinary white kind made from Whelk shells. Today, with the resurgence of shell jewelry made from *Mercenaria*, these clams once more mean money to the many dealers in novelties whose stores are found in vacation spots up and down the coast.

Mercenaria mercenaria is known by common names such as Quahog, Chowder Quahog, Cherrystone, Little Neck, Hard-shell Clam, Clam, Hard Clam, and Round Clam, depending on political location and individual size. In New Jersey restaurants, a New Englander ordering *Mercenaria* would draw a look of amazement from the waiter by asking for quahogs; to get the food you wanted, you would have to order clams, or, better, hard-shell clams. Similarly, the smallest little necks and the next largest size, cherrystone, in Rhode Island are reversed in Connecticut, where the smallest quahogs are cherrystones, and the larger hard-shell clams are little necks. In both states

(a)

(b)

7 cm
(approx. 2¾")

Mercenaria mercenaria—The Hard-Shell Clam or Quahog. (a) External view showing valves, growth rings, siphons and mantle. (b) Valves have been separated, body of the quahog is in the left valve.

the largest size is the Chowder Quahog or "chowder" (used primarily for making chowder rather than for eating raw).

By means of its powerful hatchet-shaped foot, this animal burrows on or just barely in mud, sand, or mixtures of these sediments on the flats, either just subtidally or near the lower part of the intertidal area. The ideal environment for growth of these animals apparently occurs where water made brackish by mixed fresh and ocean waters, provides reduced salinity that favors reproduction and growth, and at the same time keeps down populations of three of its most devastating predators: moon snails, oyster drills, and starfish.

Over the years, many citizens of Massachusetts, Connecticut, and Rhode Island have harvested quahogs either commercially or for private use. They have devised ingenious methods for collecting these animals. Recreational shellfishermen who have become practiced in gathering hard-shell clams have evolved a sixth sense in gathering them; they may "tread" the

7.5 cm
(approx. 3")

Mya arenaria—The Soft-shell or Steamer Clam.

bottom with their toes, bending down to scoop out the Hard-Shell Clam by hand after it has been located; they may probe the sediment directly with their fingers in the most likely places until making contact; they may use short-handled, thick-tined clam rake, with or without a small wire basket attached to the head for catching the clams as they are scratched out; and they may have one or several different-shaped inner-tube-supported baskets secured to their waist to collect the quahogs as they are gathered. Commercial (licensed) quahoggers use far more efficient apparatus, working either individually from small boats or in crews on larger boats powered by inboard motors. The former may be divided into rakers and tongers, depending on the type of gear that they use; the rakers use a so-called bull rake, a much larger and heavier version of the clam rake with the attached wire basket; the tongers balance themselves at the gunwales of an anchored boat while working their twelve- to twenty-foot-long, scissorlike, wire-cap-metal-tooth-tipped tongs into the bottom. Rakers and tongers have to be physically strong and manually dextrous to work their unwieldy collecting equipment, and bring enough quahogs into their boats to make their efforts profitable.

The dredgers work in deeper waters from thirty- to forty-foot power boats specially equipped with metal-framed mesh bags (the so-called rocking-chair dredge) that are lowered to the bottom, dragged for fifteen to thirty minutes, and brought aboard. The contents are spilled on deck for sorting by pulling the purse line. More sophisticated dredgers utilize a more effective hydraulic dredge with water jets to loosen the bottom in front of a dredge blade that can cut through the bottom to a depth of roughly four inches. Over the years sporadic friction has pitted the rakers and tongers on one side with the dredgers on the other, the former accusing the latter of harmfully digging the bay bottom until it is ruined for future fin and shellfish productivity (the scanty scientific evidence does not substantiate this claim), and of exceeding the state-prescribed limits for numbers of quahogs collected.

State law permits the amateur shell fisherman to take up to two pecks of legal-sized hard-shell clams a day. Legal-sized quahogs will not pass through a metal ring an inch and a half in diameter. Fortunately, stiff fines now await anyone caught with undersized quahogs, a misdemeanor that not too long ago was observed in the breach more than in the promise. Similar penalties are enforced against individuals taking these shellfish from habitats known to be polluted, and so advertised. Increased pollution in several areas has resulted in the prohibition of harvesting from some of the best quahog growing areas; gross pollution is now being reversed, though, and southern New England may once more become one of the best hard-shell clam-producing regions in the country.

The shell of *Mercenaria* is composed of two symmetrical halves or valves. The dorsal side of the shell has an easily recognizable brown ligament that serves as a hinge for the valves. On either side of the ligament is a swelling on each valve called the umbo or umbone, the original part of the shell of the growing clam. The growth from this area results in concentric lines of growth, more readily seen in some individuals than others, making it easier to tell the age of these more conspicuously marked animals. The markings on the inside of the shell indicate where organs were attached, the rounded scars being impressions of the muscles that operate the foot and the siphons, and open and close the valves. The distinct line connecting two of the larger scars marks the attachment of the thin, sheetlike mantle, which covers the soft parts and secretes the shell.

Two edges of the mantle are thickened and fused one above the other, forming a double tube, the incurrent and the excurrent siphons. The siphons are quite short, and are darkly pigmented. Water entering through the incurrent siphon is drawn into a large cavity containing the two pairs of thin, membranous, folded, filamented (lamellar) gills. The gills have blood vessels and are ciliated; the constantly beating hairlike cilia draw a continuous current of water through the incurrent siphon into the gill or branchial chamber, where respiratory oxygen is removed as well as the minute food particles, which are in turn directed toward the mouth. Water bearing rejected materials and metabolic wastes leave the animal through the excurrent siphon. The strength of the water currents is greatly influenced by the temperature of the environmental water, varying from greatest activity at about 22° Celsius to cessation of ciliary currents below 5° Celsius (41°F) when a sort of hibernation occurs.

The open circulatory system of *Mercenaria*, consisting of an easily accessible three-chambered heart and connecting blood vessels, has long been an excellent subject for study by physiologists, and an equally good organ for research by students in this field. It is readily perfused by salts, drugs, and other solutions, and the results of these experiments can be recorded with relatively little effort.

It is next to impossible to differentiate externally between male and female quahogs. Each adult has either a pair of testes or a pair of ovaries, which enlarge considerably during the breeding season. Spawning in this general area occurs from late June to early August, when the water temperature has risen to about 70°F (21° Celsius). An individual may spawn more than once in a season. At this time, millions of eggs and sperm are shed freely into the open water, where fertilization takes place (one female Quahog was recorded as producing 24 million eggs at one spawning). The ensuing larval stages (trochophore and veliger) are rapidly completed, and the minute young Quahog settles to the bottom in late summer, attached to a sand grain or other particle by a self-manufactured thread. Although it may be buried at this time, it eventually gets free, and following two years of growth, mostly during the warm summer months, it matures into legal collecting size by the third summer. Most of the larvae and minute young do not survive long enough to be collected, but this loss is not overly alarming, because if even 1 percent of the fertilized eggs were to survive, the bottom would literally be paved with these bivalves. In great part the combination of environmental conditions where spawning and settling occur provide for the success or lack of it in the size and quality of the Quahog population. This requirement makes some kinds of pollution particularly harmful in the continual renewal of *Mercenaria* as a commercial resource.

Two species of bivalves may be mistaken for the solid, heart-shaped, prominent-beaked, three- to five-inch by two- to four-inch-wide, Hard-Shell Clam. One is a clam that is beautifully marked, with zigzag lines of light brown on the shells and lacks the purple border within. It is three to four inches long, is most abundant in the southern part of its range, has no common name, and is called *Mercenaria mercenaria notata*. The other is the so-called Thin Venus Clam, or Widgeon, *Pitar morrhuana*, two inches by 1½ inches wide. It is dirty white, with several rust-colored or dark gray areas, the inside of the shell is bluish, and it never has a purple spot. If you ingest it, you will find it to be quite bitter.

A Local Snail That Harbors Bather's Itch

The Eastern Mud Snail, *Ilyanassa obsoleta*, belongs to a group of gastropods often called dog whelks. It is without doubt the most commonly found snail on most of the mud flats of the bays and the salt ponds in our area. In tidal mud flats, we can often see it in large numbers, either collected in shallow depressions left by the receding tides or easing along just below the film of water covering the intervening mud surfaces. Characteristic trails often indicate the presence of the mud snail in undisturbed areas. In cold weather, motion is less rapid, far fewer snails are found along the surface, and we will see greater concentrations in the deeper pools.

1.3 cm
(approx. ½″)

Ilyanassa obsoleta—The Mud Snail.

The Mud Snail is a small, dun-colored animal varying in shade from brown to black, an animal that blends well with its environment. Its conical shell has an elevated spire with six whorls, and a surface weakly reticulated (marked with a network) by many longitudinal and revolving striations that distinguish it from other snails living in the same area. The lowest whorl is larger than the rest. Very often the modest reticulations on the surface are obscured by microbial or diatom growth, to which cling particles of mud that not only disguise the shell's sculpturing, but also make the animal slippery to touch.

Adult animals are about 1¼ inches long and a half-inch across at the widest point. The opening in the largest whorl is oval, and has a short notch at its base and a row of very small, toothlike knobs just inside the outer lip. If the shell is held away from the light, you can see its purplish lining without much

difficulty. Living mud snails have a reddish brown, horny operculum or "door" to the shell, whose edges are quite smooth.

While it is gliding along the bottom, the two most obvious
characteristics of the Mud Snail are the squareness of the front
of the foot and the long, tubular anterior canal, slowly pointed
first in one direction and then in another in the apparently
never-ending search for food. At the base of this snout is the
unique file-like rasping organ or radula consisting of a ribbon
with three longitudinal rows of teeth, variously decorated with
cusps. The constant back-and-forth motion of the radula wears
away living or dead flesh, bringing the particles to the roof of
the mouth, where cilia take them to the esophagus. Here they
are bound with mucus and are carried in a viscous string
through the remainder of the digestive tract, eventually being
eliminated in the form of pellets. The number, size, and character of the teeth and the type of fecal pellets are used in
identifying the snails.

Mud snails feed almost entirely on dead and decaying materials. Probably very helpful to them is an organ between the
snout and the gills, an osphradium. This structure is analogous
to our nose, in testing the quality of the environment for the
presence of food. In mud snails, it is thought that this organ
can also help interpret the type of sediment on which the
animal is gliding.

The Mud Snail occurs from the Gulf of the St. Lawrence
River to Key West, and north along the West Coast of Florida,
being found in greatest numbers south of Cape Cod.

Mud snails drew a great deal of attention in Rhode Island
some years ago when the Rhode Island Department of Health
received many complaints from fishermen and bathers in several Narragansett Bay areas about a skin irritation apparently
resulting from exposure to waters of the Bay.

Studies by the department indicated that it was the same
kind of dermatitis produced in fresh water in this country and
abroad by one of the intermediate stages (cercaria) of the life
cycle of a blood fluke of the genus *Schistosoma*. The infection
was called "cercaria dermatitis," or bather's itch. It proved to
be caused by an animal new to science, which was given the
name *Cercaria variglandis*. Malcolm Hinchliffe of the Rhode
Island Department of Health, and Horace Stunkard of the

American Museum of Natural History determined its life history and biology.

It was determined that this blood fluke normally lives in waterfowl and wading birds. When infested birds landed on mud flats and released the blood fluke eggs in their droppings, the eggs hatched into microscopic ciliated forms that eventually found their way into the mud snails. There they developed into infective cercaria over the winter, and were released by the snails when the water turned warmer in the spring, at the same time as the waterfowl again stopped in the Bay on their way north. The blood fluke was also attracted by the warm-blooded human swimmers, but could not bore into the blood stream of this abnormal host and died in the thick skin, producing an infection.

Probably the most practical method of preventing bather's itch would be to decrease the population of the mud snails by rehabilitating the mud flats. The most efficient way of doing so would be to reduce the amount of refuse and other wastes that now pollute them, and on which a great many of the mud snails feed.

The Immigrant Snail

*T*he edible Periwinkle, *Littorina littorea*, belongs to a worldwide family of common, abundant gastropods or snails, found singly, or more often in great groups, on pilings, rocks, boulders, cobbles, and similar substrata, not only between the tides, but often as far as the reach of splashing spray from incoming rollers. Those above the low tides are well able to withstand the periods between high tides, remaining as if glued to the rocks to which they have fastened.

Periwinkles are algae eaters and vary greatly in color; the full-grown one-inch adults may be olive, brown, yellow, pale orange, gray, or, rarely, banded or entirely black. Although along parts of the coast it is the most common snail in its environment, it is not native to North America. Presumably it

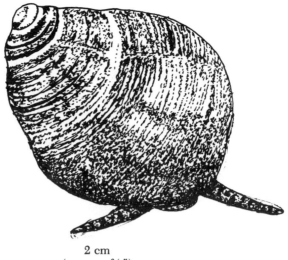

2 cm
(approx. ¾ ")

Littorina littorea—The Common Periwinkle.

was brought to this coast accidentally on a ship's bottom around the turn of the century, and, finding both shelter and food in abundance, became at once a prominent member of the North Atlantic coastal community. One group of zoologists believes that it spread to the littoral North Atlantic coast of this country by slowly working its way to Iceland, then Greenland, and finally Canada, before starting southward. Whatever their route, they are here, and they are delicious!

They have been eaten roasted, stewed, or boiled on the continent, and particularly in England, for hundreds of years. For the year 1867, it was estimated that the annual consumption of periwinkles in London was 76,000 baskets, weighing 1,900 tons, and worth upward of $50,000. That is a lot of snails. According to M. S. Lovell, Athenaeus, in his *Deipnosophists*, says ". . . of the black and red kinds of periwinkles the larger are exceedingly palatable, especially those that are caught in the spring. As a general rule, all of them are good for the stomach, and digestible when eaten with cinnamon and pepper." Periwinkles may be collected at any time of the year, but are thought to be most flavorful from September to mid-March.

In Anglo-Saxon, the Periwinkle was called "sea-snaegl" or sea snail; in Ireland, the "horse-winkle," and "shellimidy forragy," and at Belfast, "whelks"; in Cornwall, "gwean"; in France, "sabot" or wooden shoe, or "vignot," and "bigorneau"; and in Brittany, "vrelin" or "brelin." The Chinese esteem these snails and make a sort of ragout of them. Evidence of their long popularity as an article of food along the European coast is provided by the tremendous numbers found in the Danish shell mounds; they are also the most abundant shell in similar human deposits in Scotland.

It is best to collect periwinkles in sacks or in buckets from unpolluted areas where a good current runs or where there is obvious tidal flow. They can be stored for a short time, but be sure to cull the dead ones before cooking. They should never be eaten raw.

In Favor of Sea Slugs

*T*he nudibranchs or Sea Slugs are oval marine snails, from about half on inch to several inches long. Adult slugs have no shells, for although a coiled shell occurs in the embryo, it is discarded soon after birth. These sea slugs are fantastically shaped, and often brilliantly colored; some of them are thought to be among the most beautiful animals of the sea. They are prime subjects for the amateur or professional photographer.

We may locate several of these handsome animals at nearly any time of year in bays and salt ponds. They are found among the fuzzy white hydroids growing on fronds of kelp along the rocky outcrops, sliding through colonies of sea squirts that cling to pilings, or amid the ever-present sponges and moss animals. Place any of these bottom species in a large bowl or dish of seaweed, and if sea slugs are present they will make themselves known within two hours by climbing the side of the container.

Nudibranchs are almost invariably found with the kind of food they eat, each species of sea slug remaining with the food

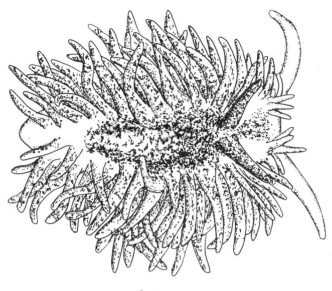

3 cm
(approx. 1¼")

Aeolidia papillosa—The Plumed Sea Slug (partially constricted).

to which it has become adapted. One of the adaptations that
first captures the eye is that different species take on the color of
the organisms on which they habitually feed. So it is that sea
slugs are jet black, purple, blue, red, brown, orange, yellow, or
white, and they may be dotted, barred, or striped. The texture
of the animal's epidermis may vary, too—from plain to warty
or papillated. Combine these unusual characteristics with the
sea slug's smooth, apparently effortless gliding on the bottom,
through the water, or on the underside of the water-surface
film, and the results are striking.

Generally speaking, the three categories of sea slugs are determined in part by the structure and appearance of their
respiratory apparatus (*nudi* means naked, and *branch* means
gill), which for all consists of exposed gills. The commonest
type have a circular fringe of flattish tentacular or scalloped
respiratory gills on the caudal (tail) end, surrounding the anus.
These are dorids or sea lemons. The aeolids or plumose sea
slugs have the entire dorsal (upper) surface covered with long,
unadorned, but colored pencil-like cerata or extensions of the

Mollusca • 189

digestive gland or liver. The third kind also has projections on the upper surface of its flattened, elongated, tapering body, but they are branching and treelike. The front margin of the third type also has bushy and fringed bumps instead of tentacles.

All sea slugs have a pair of tentacles on the head. The aeolids also have a second pair of somewhat similar thicker, twisted structures, apparently adapted for smelling, called rhinophores. Some types of nudibranchs have nematocysts or stinging cells, borrowed from the hydroids (coelenterates) on which they feed. In several species, after the hydroid is ingested, its stinging cells migrate to the tips of the sea slug's cerata, and when the animal is threatened, the cerata are waved about, offering undischarged stinging cells to the trouble-causer. It is a unique phenomenon in the animal kingdom for one animal to prey on another, digest the prey's body except for its defense cells, which are then used in turn by the predator, virtually unchanged.

There are more than fifty species of nudibranchs in these waters. Like numbers have been observed in similar lengths of coastline elsewhere, and more are being discovered from year to year by interested malacologists. Thus far, more of these animals have been recorded along North Atlantic than along Mid-Atlantic shores. Some species are numerous only at specific times of the year when their presence may be detected readily by observing their long, beautiful, and delicately coiled (usually white) egg ribbons. If carefully handled, the sea slugs may be kept alive for many months in a properly managed marine aquarium.

A related group of organisms, known as sea hares, may be found some years in late August or early September in the lower part of either passage of Narragansett Bay embayments. These hermaphroditic animals may attain a foot in length and weigh several pounds. They are washed into southern New England bays, often in large numbers, from warmer tropical Atlantic waters by eddies of the Gulf Stream. Sea hares are sea snails with two pairs of tentacles on the head, the back pair being larger and somewhat resembling the ears of a jack rabbit. They also have a transparent, soup-bowl shaped, paper-thin shell covered by folds of the mantle, and thus are, in a sense, a link between shelled snails and sea slugs.

The large brown and cream sea hares, sporadically occurring in these waters (genus *Aplysia*) ingest algae, aided by their jaws and rows of backward-pointing teeth (radula), and pass them into three stomachs, where they are ground still smaller by large, horny teeth. When handled they may give off a beautiful purple dye, which is thought to act as an escape cloud and to paralyze or somehow offend would-be predators.

Sea hares not only creep and glide like other snails, but have broad lateral extensions of their feet (parapodia) large enough to enfold their dorsal surface completely. In some parts of the world, the parapodia are stewed or broiled and esteemed as delicacies.

The North Atlantic Coast's Largest Edible Snails

Three of the best-known whelks, or, as the large species are sometimes locally called, conchs, can be found just below the low tide limit or in slightly deeper waters. There is the Waved Whelk, *Buccinium undatum*, slightly more than three inches high, which lives along the Atlantic Coast from New Jersey to Greenland, and also in Europe, where it grows larger than it does here; the Channeled Whelk, *Busycon canaliculatum*, up to seven inches high, distributed from Cape Cod to Florida; and the largest snail growing in these waters, the Knobbed Whelk, *Busycon carica*, which commonly reaches a height of nine inches.

The Waved Whelk ordinarily lives on mussel beds, where it can be found at dead low water, or it can be caught by tying a dead fish in a bag of cheesecloth and anchoring this bait among rocks near the low-tide line. Its shell has six convex whorls, each with about twelve obliquely undulating ribs covered by fine spiral ridges or by prominent raised lines, a char-

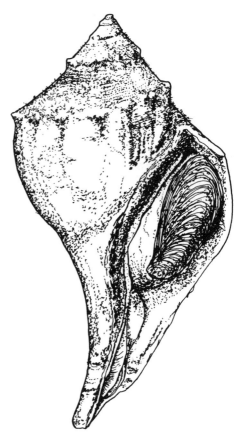

11 cm
(approx. 4⅜″)

Busycon carica—The Knobbed Whelk or Knobby Conch.

acteristic that gives this gastropod its common name. In the living animal, the outer covering of the shell is somewhat velvety, the shell opening (aperture) is usually lined with light yellow or white, and the horny plate that closes the aperture (operculum) never seems to close entirely. The aperture characteristically has a wide notch at the lower side about as long as the spire, and forms a short, wide canal. The body of the animal inside the shell is white, blotched and streaked with black.

The eggs of the Waved Whelk are laid in yellowish capsules, hundreds of eggs to a capsule, each about the size and shape of a garden pea. The egg capsules overlap each other, and are sometimes laid in such numbers as to form a mass about the size of the palm of one's hand. The young hatch and escape from the capsules as minute copies of their parents and rest on the bottom. It is said that sailors used these egg clusters to wash their hands, and they became known in some quarters as "seawash balls." Empty balls may be found sometimes along high-tide line, still fastened to the stalk of algae around which they were originally deposited. If all the young whelks have not escaped, the rattle produced by shaking the capsule briskly will reveal their presence. The Waved Whelk is usually carnivorous, living mostly on small bivalves and annelids (segmented round worms); it becomes the fisherman's anathema when it steals the bait from lobster pots and from cod lines.

The Channeled Whelk has a thin, yellow or fawn-colored shell, covered in life with a hairy periostracum (thin layer covering outside of shell). The outer lip of the shell is thin, the largest or body whorl (lowest whorl) is very prominent, and carries along its outer edge a beading whose shape and size depend on the age of the animal. This whorl is prolonged below into a narrow, nearly straight tubular canal. Commonly a deep, channel-like groove lies at the junction between the whorls of the shell. As might be expected in an animal of this size, the operculum is large; it is also rough and grayish-brown.

The egg case of this animal is familiar to many people because it is a common object on beaches at certain times of the year. It consists of a "book" of flattened, membranous capsules almost the size of a half dollar attached at one end of a tough, cordlike structure. The eggs are laid in these upright-edged, parchmentlike, disk-shaped capsules about an inch in diameter. The string may have as many as a hundred capsules, and may be more than three feet long; sometimes it may curve on itself, and sometimes it may get washed far up on the beach and dry out before the young whelks can eat their way through. Then the shells of the young dead whelks will rattle if we shake the string. This animal and its close relative, the Knobbed Whelk, are carnivorous, living mostly on other mollusks, worms, nemertines, and other likely prey. Both species are commonly sold in Italian fish markets, their feet forming the main ingredient of a delicious dish called scungili.

The Knobbed Whelk has a large, pear-shaped, heavy, ash-colored shell that shows longitudinal streaks of brownish purple when the animal is young. The row of low knobs along the outer edge of the body whorl gives this species its common name. Unlike the Channeled Whelk, it has no periostracum, the expanded body whorl forms an oval aperture with a long and open canal, the shell sutures are shallow, and the inside of the large opening varies from gleaming yellow to bright brick red. It is relatively common in some places in shallow water, and very often living specimens are tossed or washed on the beaches by storm waves, where the shell remains to be picked up by beachcombers after the animal has died and its soft parts have dried up and disappeared. The eggs of this species are laid in a similar manner, and have essentially the same shape as those of the Channeled Whelk, except that the capsules are double-edged.

Both of these giant whelks or conchs have a large fleshy body, with a broad foot on which they are able to move with surprising rapidity. As they glide, the shell is directed with the canal extended upward and forward so that the siphon protected within constantly projects its enclosed incurrent and excurrent tubes ahead of the animal. The head, carrying a pair of stout, tapering tentacles, with an eye at the lower outer edge of each tentacle, is beneath the siphon. A characteristically elephant-trunklike, constantly moving, long proboscis with a typical snail ribbon of rasping teeth inside the terminal mouth projects forward beneath the head. This apparatus is deadly for oysters and other bivalves. According to William Amos, the whelk grabs an oyster with its muscular foot, then whacks its own siphonal canal against the leading edge of the closed oyster. After the oyster shell is broken, the whelk inserts its canal into the break, and by twisting, cracks off enough of both oyster valves to thrust its proboscis inside and ingest the soft body of its victim. A variant of this method of invasion is for the whelk to grasp a clam or mussel with its foot and break its victim's shell with repeated heavy blows by its body whorl. These animals also use their ribbon of rasping, file-like teeth (radula) to bore neat, round holes through the shells of a variety of mollusks before sucking out their contents.

Whelks and conchs are considered to be great delicacies not only up and down the coasts of Europe but also in the Bahamas and other islands of the West Indies, where one can readily obtain in the local restaurants delicious conch chowder, conch salads, and fried conchs.

Gastropods deserving great fame,
Call them whelks, conchs, or snails,
*   it's the same:*
Their feet ground in a chopper
Or broiled with wine as a sopper
Will gain lasting gourmet acclaim.

The Squid—Denizen of the Sea and Delicacy for the Diner

The Squid is a mollusk, in a group called Cephalopoda, meaning head feet, which also includes different kinds of octopus, cuttlefish, sepias, the Curly and Paper Argonauts, and the owner of the shell so valuable to collectors, the Pearly Nautilus. The cephalopods are among the most highly evolved invertebrates. Squid are found most commonly off the New England coast in relatively shallow waters from twelve to around a hundred feet down, where they are caught in the nets of fishermen. During the spring months, they come fairly close to low-tide line along the shore, where they deposit their eggs by the thousands in bunches of fingerlike gelatinous capsules cemented to rocks or other types of hard substratum on the bottom.

It is difficult to see squid in their native habitat except by strong electric light at night when they may wander close to docks and wharfs. When observed in aquaria, their grace of form and movement, the large, humanlike eyes, and the constant change of color that seems to glide along their bodies like passing shadows are striking.

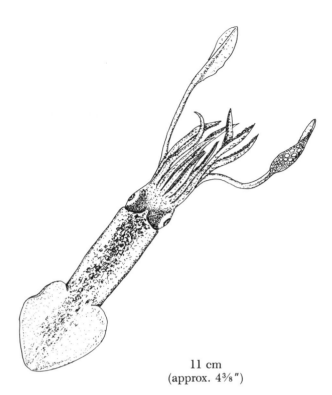

11 cm
(approx. 4⅜")

Ommastrephes illecebrosa—The Sea Arrow or the Flying Squid, found from Cape Cod Bay northward.

Squid are streamlined, and are able to swim faster backward than forward. They manage this feat by drawing water through a large opening surrounding the head, then forcing it through a small tube or funnel by muscular contraction of the body covering or mantle. This is true hydraulic jet propulsion, and by directing the funnel forward or backward the animal can progress in either direction. Its fins can be used for swimming, but are more often applied in holding its position. The ten tentacles or arms of a squid, a long time ago mistakenly thought to be feet, extend from the head and are used in capturing food and in mating.

The only hard shell in the Squid, which indicates kinship with the mollusk, is a light, horny, transparent, pen-shaped structure, aptly called the pen, along the animal's back. This part stiffens the animal's body and supports it. A large ink-producing gland empties into a sac with an ejection apparatus that opens near the anus. The gland secretes a black fluid containing a melanin pigment (the same chemical that colors our skin). When alarmed, the ink sac expels a jet-black ink through the funnel, clouding the water and hiding the Squid at least temporarily from its enemies.

The local squid are small species from one to two feet long, but the so-called Giant Squid in the open ocean reach a length of 66 feet and a weight of 42 tons. These giant invertebrates are a favorite in the diet of the great sperm whales; their smaller relatives grace human tables in many parts of the world.

Recipes

When the Tide is Out, Dinner is Served

Very few of the mollusks or crustaceans in the marine bays and ponds of this coast cannot be eaten. Nearly all are easy to collect on pilings, between tides, in patches of Eelgrass, on mud or sand flats, covering submerged rocks and logs, or just below low-tide line. Many of them are best eaten raw, all can be cooked, and for most you can interchange the same kinds of animals in the recipes without loss of flavor, texture, or final appearance. The table indicates kinds of animals, their names, locations, and methods of preparation.

By and large, collecting these delicacies offers little problem. You can walk along the shore with a bucket at low tide and simply pick up periwinkles, whelks, mussels, and an occasional oyster. Quahogs and steamer clams, enough for one meal, may be dug in sand-mud flats as a family enterprise with shovel, clam rake, or plumber's helper. Crabs of all kinds, bay scallops, and shrimp may be netted from a dinghy or other small boat. A word passed along to friendly dredgers or fishermen may bring back sea urchins, crabs, mantis shrimp, deckers, and similar beasts. The only items on the list that may have to be purchased are squid (either fresh or freshly frozen) and lobsters. The best shrimping results from actively swishing a fine-meshed, long-handled dip net through beds of eelgrass, either on foot or from a sturdy dinghy.

Many people wonder how nutritious these marine organisms are. All those investigated have been shown to be generally superior in mineral, vitamin, and trace elements to foods that most people consider more normal table fare. Weight for weight, the oyster is the most nutritious natural food known.

Before using the recipes given for many of these animals, you may want to look over these general rules for their preparation. Perhaps the most important thing to remember is that all shellfish must be cleaned before you do anything else with them. Bivalves such as mussels and oysters, and univalves such as limpets and periwinkles, must be scrubbed under running cold water before they are opened. Generally you can open them by inserting a thin, sturdy, sharp-bladed knife along a side away from the hinge, and then working the knife around to the hinge, twisting in both directions to cut the muscles holding the shell together. Another method is to steam the animals in a deep pot in about an inch of water; they will open in a few minutes, and the meat may then be removed for further preparation. If the shells of oysters and mussels have "beards," take these off.

If you intend to eat limpets, periwinkles, and whelks without additional attention, wash and scrub them in running cold water, then put them in a saucepan of cold water to soak for about ten minutes. Shake the pan until they all pull back into the shells, pour off the cold water, and cover the animals with boiling, salted water. Boil them quickly for up to twenty minutes, remove from the shells, and serve in white sauce with chopped parsley.

Crabs should be boiled in a saucepan in water seasoned with salt, pepper, parsley, and chopped onion. Add ½ cup vinegar and 1 teaspoonful cayenne pepper to every 2 quarts of water. Put in the crabs and boil rapidly for five minutes, then simmer for fifteen minutes more. When they are cool, remove claws and legs, cracking them with pliers or a hammer, and take out the meat. Take off the parts that folds under the body, and at this junction insert a knife between the shells, at the same time twisting to separate them. You can then remove the meat.

Place lobster in cold, salted water (1 tablespoon of salt to 1 quart of water), or sea water slowly brought to a strong boil. You can take the animal from the pot and eat it at once, or cool it and dissect it much as you would a crab, except that you remove the tail from the body and remove the meat in one entire piece. The only parts of a lobster that should not be eaten, in addition to the shell, are the baglike stomach and the featherlike gills. The pistachio-green, so-called liver, and the brilliant red "coral" or ovary are delicacies and should not be discarded.

When eating shrimps and prawns, tear or cut off the head and thorax (the part bearing the legs), and peel off and discard the nearly transparent head covering. You can remove the small back streak (intestine), if you want to but it is not really necessary. When using frozen Shrimps or Prawns, do not thaw them until you are ready to cook them.

Wash Squid thoroughly in cold water, cut the head off and discard it, and rub off the outer membrane and throw it away. For most recipes, make a straight slit with a sharp knife the length of the body and remove both the cartilage or "pen" and the digestive tract.

Sea urchins must also be washed; take special care to avoid being speared by the movable spines during this procedure. Use a pair of sharp scissors to cut through the thin, solid, but brittle shell at its widest circumference. Pull the two resultant pieces gently apart. If the animal is a male (sexes are practically impossible to distinguish even for the most experienced marine biologist), the contents will be white or light gray, and we discard the animal. If it is a female, a serpentine orange mass of minute eggs will be plainly visible. We can scoop these out and spread them on toast.

In preparing seafood dishes, avoid overwashing in running water, or overcooking to dryness. Remember that white wine is often an excellent substitute for water, and that a sprinkling of fresh herbs before serving enhances most dishes.

"You must reflect carefully beforehand with whom you are to eat and drink, rather than what you are to eat and drink. For a dinner or meals without the company of a friend is like the life of a lion or a wolf."   Epicarus

Common Name	Scientific Name	Where Found	How Eaten
Oyster	*Cassostrea virginica*	On hard objects in the shallows	Raw or cooked
Quahog	*Mercenaria mercenari*	Sand-mud bottoms	Raw or cooked
Steamer Clam	*Mya arenaria*	Mud, mud-sand bottoms	Cooked
Decker (boat shells)	*Crepidula fornicata*	Stacked on hard objects	Raw
Moon Shell	*Natica,* sp.	Intertidal sand flats	Cooked
Razor Clam	*Ensis directus*	Intertidal sand beaches	Cooked
Surf Clam	*Spisula solidissima*	Sand flats exposed at low tide	Cooked
Bay Scallop	*Arqopecten irradians*	In or near Eelgrass beds	Raw or cooked
Sea Scallop	*Placopecten magellenicus*	In deep water, off-shore	Cooked
Chiton	*Chaetopleura opiculata*	In shallow water on cobbles	Cooked
Cockle	*Cardium islandicum*	In deeper water, offshore	Cooked
Edible Mussel	*Mytilus edulis*	In clusters on hard objects near low-tide line	Cooked
Conch or Whelk	*Buccinium undatum*	Near low tide line in bays	Cooked
Periwinkle	*Littorina littorea*	Commonest snail on hard objects between and above tide lines	Cooked
Limpet	*Acmaea testitudinalis*	On rocks in shallow water	Cooked
Sea Hare	*Aplysia* sp.	On large algae in September	Cooked
King or Horseshoe Crab	*Limulus polyphemus*	Intertidal sloping sand beaches	Cooked
Rock Crab	*Cancer irroratus*	Among rocks and in sand	Cooked
Jonah Crab	*Cancer borealis*	Among rocks and in sand	Cooked
Blue Crab	*Callinectes sapidus*	Swimming in shallow ocean or brackish waters	Cooked
Lady Crab	*Ovalipes ocellatus*	On sandy intertidal beaches	Cooked
Spider Crab	*Libinia* sp.	Mud flats and oyster beds and elsewhere	Cooked
Green Crab	*Carcinides meanas*	Among rocks in shallow water	Cooked
Mantis or Ghost Shrimp	*Squilla empusa*	In shallow burrows in mud	Cooked
Shrimp or Prawn	Many species	Most easily netted in Eelgrass	Cooked
Lobster	*Homarus americanus*	In deeper water, rocky bottom	Cooked
Squid	*Loligo paeliei*	Swimming	Cooked
Sea Urchin	*Arbacia punctulata*	Low water to 120 fathoms	Eggs eaten raw
Green Urchin	*Strongylocentrotus drobachiensis*	Low water to 650 fathoms	Eggs eaten raw

CHITON

Chiton Soup

2	quarts washed chitons	1	garlic clove
1	cup water	¼	cup celery
2	tablespoons butter		salt and pepper to taste
1	onion	½	cup white wine
1	potato		chopped parsley
1	carrot		buttered toast rounds

Put washed chitons in a kettle with water and steam covered for 10 minutes after the water starts boiling. Strain and save the broth. When the chitons are cool enough to handle, remove the meat and discard the shells.

Melt butter in a heavy frying pan or kettle. Add chiton meat, onion, potato, carrot, garlic clove, and celery, all finely chopped, cover and sauté until the onion is transparent but not browned. Combine enough water with the chiton broth to make 1 quart and add to the vegetables. Season with salt and freshly ground black pepper. Simmer 30 minutes, then add wine. Dish into bowls, sprinkle with chopped parsley, and float a round of buttered toast on each serving. Serves 6.

CRAB

Crab Cocktail

2	cups fresh crabmeat	1	tablespoon lemon juice
3	tablespoons catsup	1	tablespoon
2	tablespoons horseradish		Worcestershire sauce
		⅛	tablespoon red pepper sauce

Mix catsup, horseradish, lemon juice, salt, Worcestershire sauce, and hot sauce, and season with salt to taste. Chill thoroughly. Flake crabmeat and add. Serve in chilled cocktail glasses. Serves 4.

Crabmeat Omelette

1½	cups fresh crabmeat	⅔	cup grated cheese
3	tablespoons butter		salt and pepper to taste
3	tablespoons flour	½	cup milk
1	cup milk	8	eggs

Make cream sauce using butter, flour, 1 cup milk, and cheese. Season to taste. Add crabmeat, set aside, and keep hot. Beat together eggs, ½ cup milk, and salt and pepper. Pour into heavy, well-buttered skillet; as mixture cooks, lift it with broad knife to let raw part run under it. When browned, place in oven until well set. Pour part of crabmeat sauce into the omelette, roll up, put on a hot platter, and pour the remaining sauce around it. Garnish and serve at once. Serves 8.

Deviled Crabs

12	cooked hard-shelled crabs	1	teaspoon dry mustard
		½	teaspoon horseradish
4	tablespoons butter	1	teaspoon salt
2	tablespoons flour	1	cup milk
1	tablespoon minced parsley	2	hard-boiled eggs, minced
2	teaspoons lemon juice	½	cup buttered bread crumbs

Remove meat from the hard-shelled crabs; reserve 6 of the upper shells and wash them thoroughly. Melt butter in a saucepan, add flour, stir until smooth; add parsley, lemon juice, mustard, horseradish, salt, and milk, stir until smooth, and add crabmeat and minced eggs. Mix thoroughly, and put into the crab shells. Sprinkle with bread crumbs, and bake in a hot oven for about 10 minutes. Serves 6.

Crab Supreme

1⅓	cups fresh crabmeat	2½	cups milk
4	tablespoons shortening	⅓	cup chopped cooked celery
6	tablespoons flour		
½	teaspoon salt	⅔	cup browned small mushrooms
¼	teaspoon paprika		mashed potatoes

Melt shortening. Add flour. When the two are well blended, add salt, paprika, and milk. Cook slowly and stir constantly until thick and creamy. Add rest of the ingredients and heat thoroughly. Serve with mashed potato border. Serves 4.

Curried Crabmeat

1½	cups fresh crabmeat	3	tablespoons flour
2	tablespoons butter	1	cup chicken broth (or
1	teaspoon finely chopped		other good stock)
	green onion		salt and pepper to taste
⅔	tablespoon curry		
	powder		

Cook onion in butter 3 minutes. Add flour mixed with curry powder and chicken stock. Bring to boiling point and add crabmeat. Season to taste. Serves 4.

Crabmeat Salad

1	pound fresh crabmeat	salt and pepper
1	heart of lettuce	mayonnaise
juice of one lemon		

Clean lettuce and arrange 6 nests about 4 inches across. Mix crabmeat, lemon juice, seasoning as desired, and enough mayonnaise to hold the crabmeat together when pressed into a small cup. Invert contents of the cup into a lettuce nest and repeat. Put a spoonful of mayonnaise over each. Mix no more than 1 cup of chopped celery, apple, hard-boiled egg, olives, and so on with the crabmeat if desired. Serves 6.

Fried Soft-Shelled Crabs

Use soft-shell local blue crabs, green crabs, lady crabs, or cancer crabs. Purge live crabs in a salt solution (1 tablespoon table salt to a quart of water) for a few minutes. Drain, dry, and fry in deep fat until nicely browned. Serve on well-buttered toast, with tartar or other sauce. The entire crab is edible.

OYSTER CRAB

Mussel and oyster crabs can be sautéed in butter, or cooked in batter, or fried, and when they are served in the latter way, they are said to rival the finest broiled soft-shell crabs. Pea crabs can also be cooked with the hosts and eaten together with them. Gathering enough of these small delicacies does, however, limit their appearance on most dining tables, because of the time it takes.

Oyster Crab Newburg

Joe Cannon's column in the *Washington Post* (February 11, 1972) offered this recipe, serving four, for Oyster Crab Newburg. Mussel crabs would probably work equally well.

1	cup oyster crabs	1	tablespoon flour
1	cup mushroom caps, coarsely chopped		salt, cayenne, and nutmeg to taste
⅓	cup sherry	¾	cup heavy cream
4	tablespoons (½ stick) butter	2	egg yolks, slightly beaten
		1	tablespoon brandy

Mix together the chopped mushroom caps, oyster crabs, and sherry. Cover and let stand 1 hour. Melt butter in a saucepan. When it bubbles, add sherry mixture and simmer 8 minutes. Stir in flour. Cook 2 minutes more. Season with salt, cayenne, and nutmeg to taste. Add cream and heat through. Just before serving, stir in egg yolks, then brandy. Taste and adjust seasonings if necessary. Serves 4.

CRAYFISH

Crayfish Salad

3	quarts large crayfish	1	tablespoon vinegar
	cayenne pepper	1	tablespoon
1½	tablespoons gelatin		Worcestershire sauce
1	large can tomatoes	1	tablespoon onion juice
	or same amount of	⅛	teaspoon pepper
	fresh, peeled tomatoes	6	olives, minced
	salt to taste	½	cup minced celery
	juice of half lemon	1	minced green pepper
		1	tablespoon prepared
			horseradish

Cook the scrubbed crayfish 5 or 6 minutes in rapidly boiling salted water to which you have added a dash of cayenne. Drain, cool, remove meat from tail, and chop fine. Also take out the black intestinal tract. Cook tomatoes to a pulp and press pulp through a sieve to make a pint of purée.

Soak gelatin in half a cup of cold water 15 minutes, then pour over the hot tomato purée and add salt, lemon juice, vinegar, and Worcestershire sauce, onion juice, and black pepper, and a small amount of cayenne pepper.

Stir all together, and cool. Set in refrigerator to partially congeal. Beat well, add all the other ingredients, mix vigorously, turn into a mold, dip in cold water, and put in the refrigerator to set. Unmold, cut in thin slices, serve on shredded lettuce, topped with mayonnaise and garnished with large claws.

Mole Crab Chowder

1½	pounds live mole crabs	½	teaspoon uncooked
2	slices uncooked bacon,		coriander, minced
	chopped	1	cup noodles, spaghetti,
2	large red onions,		rice, or diced potatoes
	chopped		white or toasted wheat flour
1	tablespoon vegetable		salt and freshly ground
	oil		pepper to taste
4	cups water	1	tablespoon butter

Wash the crabs thoroughly in a colander with a heavy stream of cold water from faucet or spray. Place the bacon in a kettle and on low heat cook 12 minutes. Add onions and gently fry until golden brown. Steam crabs with 2 cups of water about 20 minutes (until tender) in a covered pan. After removing pan from stove and mashing the crabs thoroughly with a wood or metal potato masher, strain the mixture through cheesecloth, retaining the broth and discarding the crabs.

Add the bacon-onion liquid (with the onion but minus the bacon bits) to the broth; also add the coriander and the remaining 2 cups of water. Heat the broth, add any one of the noodle or other ingredients with sufficient additional water to cook whatever has been added. Further thicken as needed with the flour. Flavor to taste with salt and pepper, and dot each serving with butter. Serves 6.

LOBSTER

According to Linz, Fuchs, and Troup in their excellent cookbook, *The Lobster's Fine Kettle of Fish*, published by Citadel Press, two excellent lobster dishes are Lobster Cocktail with Cognac and Epicurean Lobster Newburg.

Lobster Cocktail with Cognac

2	cups chopped, cooked lobster meat	2	teaspoons chopped chives
1	tablespoon chili sauce	½	cup mayonnaise
2	teaspoons lemon juice	2	tablespoons cognac
1	teaspoon minced fresh parsley	salt and pepper to taste	

Combine all the ingredients, folding lobster meat in last. Chill at least an hour and serve in cocktail dishes. Serves 2 to 6, depending on the size of the dish.

Epicurean Lobster Newburg

3	boiled 1½-pound lobsters	1½	cups light cream
¼	cup butter	4	egg yolks, well beaten
½	teaspoon paprika	1	tablespoon cognac
½	cup sherry		

Remove meat from lobsters and cut into slices ¾ inch thick. Sauté meat in butter 3 or 4 minutes. Add paprika and stir well. Add sherry and cook until wine has almost completely disappeared. Combine cream and egg yolks and stir slowly into lobster. Stir constantly until sauce is smooth and thick. Add cognac. Serve on hot buttered toast points, garnished with coral from the lobster. Serves 6.

MUSSELS

Fried Mussels

edible mussels
flour

olive oil
salt and pepper
garlic sauce or Hollandaise sauce

Scrub the mussels thoroughly. Wash in clear water. Place in a deep kettle without water and cover. Cook over high heat until the shells open (four to five minutes). Remove the meat from the shells, and roll in flour seasoned with salt and pepper. Fry in olive oil until golden brown. Drain on absorbent paper and serve at once, with garlic or Hollandaise sauce.

Mussels with Tomatoes

edible mussels
tomatoes

bread crumbs
salt and pepper

Steam open the mussels, remove from the shells, and for each pound of mussel meat take 2 tomatoes, dice them, and fry them in a little butter with a tablespoon of bread crumbs; season with salt and pepper. When done, add the mussels with a little of the liquor in which they were cooked, mix, and serve hot.

Mussel Casserole

This surprisingly excellent recipe can be made precisely like an ordinary chicken and noodle casserole except that we substitute 1 pound of cleaned Mussels for the chicken. If, after heating it for 40 minutes in a 350° oven, it becomes too dry, pour undiluted canned mushroom soup over it to remedy the drought.

Stuffed Mussels

3	dozen edible mussels	1	tomato, peeled and
3	large onions, minced		minced
1	cup olive oil	2	tablespoons pine nuts
¾	cup long-grain rice, washed and drained		generous ½ teaspoon allspice
			salt and pepper to taste

Scrub outsides of the mussel shells. Rinse. Open with the point of a sharp knife, and remove any hair. Rinse thoroughly. Loosen joints so that the shells will remain closed after stuffing. Sauté the minced onions in olive oil in a saucepan until transparent. Add the rest of the ingredients and mix thoroughly. When cool enough to handle, place a spoonful of stuffing in each shell (not too full, to allow for expansion of rice). Close the shells, and place in layers in a deep pan. Cover with a glass pie plate, and pour two cups of water over the plate. Cover the pan, and simmer over low heat 1½ to 1¾ hours, or until rice is cooked. Remove from pan and cool. Place in refrigerator to chill. Serve with lemon. Serves 6.

OYSTERS

Roasted Oysters

oysters   melted butter

Many gourmets firmly believe that after the raw state, the next best way to eat oysters is to roast them on a grate over glowing coals. Scrub the oysters and place them side by side, deep shell down, on the grate. They may be eaten immediately after they have steamed themselves open; spike them directly from the shell, dip them in parsley butter or brown butter, and pop them into your mouth. Let them cook a bit longer in their own juice, and they will be drier and assume an unbeatable smoky flavor.

Oyster Pan Roast on Toast

12	oysters, shucked	1	tablespoon sherry
salt and pepper to taste		toast	
1	tablespoon butter	parsley	
½	cup cream		

Put oysters (1 serving) in saucepan and season with salt and pepper and butter. Cook over moderate heat until nicely poached. Add cream and sherry. Put oysters on toast, pour the broth over them, and sprinkle with chopped parsley.

Vary this recipe with 3 tablespoons Worcestershire sauce, dash of Tabasco, and a tablespoon of chili sauce instead of the cream and sherry. It makes a hotter broth. Serves 1.

Angels on Horseback

1	pint select fresh oysters in their juice	⅛	teaspoon paprika
12	slices bacon, cut in thirds	2	tablespoons parsley, chopped
½	teaspoon salt	3	dozen plain, long toothpicks
½	teaspoon freshly ground pepper		

Drain oysters (if you are using frozen oysters, thaw and drain). Lay each oyster across a piece of bacon and sprinkle with seasonings and chopped parsley. Roll the bacon around the oyster carefully and fasten with a toothpick. Place the oysters on a rack in a shallow baking pan and bake in a hot oven at 450°F for 8 to 10 minutes or until bacon is crisp on both sides. Makes approximately 36 "Angels."

Recipes • 213

SHRIMP

Canape of Shrimp

anchovy butter
minced cooked shrimp
minced green pepper
minced red pepper
minced apple

mayonnaise
thin slices tomato
toast slices
chopped egg

Spread anchovy butter on toast cut into fancy shapes. Combine minced shrimp, red and green peppers, and some apple; blend together with a little mayonnaise; spread on thin slices of tomatoes, lay on toast, decorate with chopped eggs, bits of shrimp, and peppers.

Shrimp Cocktail

juice of ½ lemon
8 drops Tabasco sauce
1 can shrimp

½ teaspoon vinegar
½ teaspoon horseradish
½ teaspoon tomato catsup

Mix together. Serve in thoroughly chilled glasses.

Creole Gumbo

1 large can shrimp
2 dozen oysters
1 chicken
1 onion, sliced
1 tablespoon flour

several pieces of ham
1½ quarts water
chopped parsley
salt
strong pepper

Cut chicken in pieces and fry in hot vegetable oil. Add onion, flour, oysters, and ham, and fry until brown. Add water and simmer 1 hour. Season with parsley, salt, and pepper. Add shrimp and cook 15 minutes longer; then pour at once into a tureen, and add boiled rice.

Shrimp in Blankets

shrimp
milk
salt and pepper

thin bacon slices
toasted wafers
quartered lemon

Soak shrimp in milk, with seasoning, wrap them in slices of bacon; broil until brown on both sides. Serve on toasted wafers, with lemon quarters.

French-Fried Shrimp

1½	pounds shrimp	1	clove garlic, minced
2	tablespoons melted butter	⅛	teaspoon paprika
1	cup chopped onion	1	pint stewed tomatoes
1	cup chopped green pepper	salt and pepper	

Peel shrimp, wash, and remove dark intestinal tract. Cook onion, green pepper, and garlic in butter until pepper is tender, then add tomato and seasonings and cook over high heat 5 minutes. Add shrimp and cook 10 minutes longer. Serves 4-6.

SEAWEED

According to the experts and J. C. Madlener's *Seavegetable Book*, probably the definitive work on preparing seaweeds for the table, the best methods for cooking seaweeds to preserve their nutritive value are blanching, steaming, and stir frying. For best results, parboil kelps (such as *Alaria* and *Laminaria*) before stir-frying, sautéing, or preparing them as tempura. If you use salt, add it only a few minutes before removing the food from the heat. When you prepare soups or stews with marine algae, do not let the seaweeds soak overnight in the liquid; eat these dishes shortly after making them. Like garden lettuce, seaweeds will wilt if not refrigerated, and foods prepared with these algae should be kept cool if they are to be held for any length of time. Use either freshly collected live material or the sun-dried seaweeds available at health-food stores. Consult the *Seavegetable Book* for additional helpful information and suggestions.

Irish Moss Mousse

½	cup Irish moss	¼	cup pure grade A
1	pint milk		maple syrup
½	teaspoon pure vanilla	1	egg yolk, stiffly beaten
	extract	1	egg white, stiffly beaten
		1	pint, whipping cream, stiffly beaten

Cover the Irish moss with cold water and soak it no longer than 15 minutes; remove debris; drain and remove any additional foreign material. Tie the Irish moss in a 10-inch square of cheesecloth. Put milk and vanilla in top of a double boiler, suspend the cheesecloth bag in the milk mixture, and gradually bring the liquid to a boil. Reduce the heat and slow simmer, at the same time stirring and regularly pressing the bag against the side of the container with the spoon. After 20 minutes, remove the mixture from the heat and discard the bag.

Let stand about 5 minutes, then add the maple syrup (raw wild honey may be substituted), pour it into a bowl, stir the beaten egg yolk into the warm mixture, and fold in the beaten egg white. Ladle the mixture into dessert dishes, cover, and refrigerate. Before serving, top with the whipped cream (which may be sweetened with confectioners sugar and a few drops of vanilla). Serves 4.

Mackerel in Sea Lettuce

4	adult medium to large	salt
	fresh Atlantic mackerel	cider vinegar
8	large fronds of sea	batter for frying
	lettuce	

Behead and gut the fish, open them out flat from below, and with a sharp filleting knife, remove the backbones cleanly. Rinse the fish thoroughly in cold water, and blot them on paper towels.

Soak the fish for up to an hour in a mixture of 4 parts salt water to 1 part cider vinegar, to which you might add a clove of garlic or a bag of commercial crayfish, shrimp, and crab boil. Thoroughly dry each piece of fish separately and wrap it completely in as much sea lettuce as it takes. Dip in batter for frying, or deep-fry without batter. Serves 4.

Sea Lettuce Soup

½	cup sea lettuce	½	cup cooked chicken, diced
½	cup small white onions, diced	½	cup canned green peas
½	cup carrots, chopped	2	teaspoons soy sauce
2	quarts water	½	teaspoon freshly ground pepper
			salt to taste

Wash and clean sea lettuce by gently rinsing in ambient-temperature fresh water, checking carefully for both live and dead foreign material.

In soup pot or kettle, boil onions and carrots in water about 20 minutes, cut sea lettuce into 1-inch squares, and add to boiling water; then add chicken and simmer 5 minutes. Add the peas and let stand 2 minutes. Add the seasonings, salt to taste, and serve hot. Serves 6–8.

SQUID

Squid in Its Ink

6	small squid	½	cup boiling water
1	onion, chopped	1	cup cooked rice
2	garlic cloves, minced	2	tomatoes, chopped
½	cup olive oil		salt and pepper
			minced parsley

Clean and wash squid, reserving the ink sacs, and cut the bodies and tentacles into pieces. Sauté onion and garlic in olive oil until onion is lightly browned. Add squid and boiling water and simmer 15 minutes. Add rice, tomatoes, and ink from the sacs and mix well. Cover and cook over a low flame for about 20 minutes, or until the squid is tender. The cooking time will depend on the size of the squid. Add salt and pepper to taste and sprinkle generously with parsley. Serves 4.

Squid Cacciatore Ranger Hall

12	small squid	½	teaspoon pepper
¼	clove garlic, minced	¼	teaspoon oregano
⅓	pound mushrooms, sliced	6	tablespoons olive oil
4	slices bread, crumbled	¼-⅓	pint prepared spaghetti meat sauce
1	tablespoon parsley, chopped		toast points
¾	teaspoon salt		

Clean, skin, and wash fresh or thawed fresh-frozen squid. Cut off the tentacles, remove the viscera, and discard. With a sharp knife, slice the bodies into strips 1 to 1½ inches wide and set aside. Mix garlic, mushrooms, bread, parsley, salt, pepper, oregano, and olive oil. Arrange around the center of a cast-iron skillet. In the center of the skillet pour your favorite spaghetti meat sauce and turn the heat to low. Place the squid strips in the warm spaghetti sauce for about 5 minutes. Mix in other ingredients, turn heat up slightly, and cook 10 to 15 minutes, stirring occasionally until squid is white, slightly curled, and tender. Serve on toast points. This recipe was developed and used by the class in invertebrate zoology at the University of Rhode Island. Serves 6.

Small Squid Genoa

3	pounds small squid	½	pound mushrooms, sliced
2	onions, chopped		
6	tablespoons olive oil	½	teaspoon rosemary
2	tablespoons minced parsley	4	tablespoons tomato puree
1	clove garlic, minced	1	cup water

Clean, skin, and wash squid and cut them into serving pieces. Sauté onions in olive oil until they are lightly browned. Add parsley, garlic, mushrooms, and rosemary, and cook 5 minutes. Add the squid, tomato puree, and water, cover, and cook gently about 40 minutes, or until the squid are tender. Serves 4.

Squid Sailor Style

4	squid	½	cup dry bread crumbs
3	medium onions	1	egg
1	garlic clove	½	cup sliced or chopped
1	teaspoon parsley		parsley
2	tablespoons olive oil	salt and pepper to taste	

Wash squid and remove head and tentacles, reserving tentacles, but do not cut body of squid open lengthwise. Boil ½ hour in salted water. Chop onion, tentacles, garlic, and parsley fine and sauté in olive oil. Add this mixture to dry bread crumbs. Then add the egg and mix well. When squid are cooked, stuff with bread-crumb mixture. Simmer tomatoes 5 minutes in a saucepan. Place stuffed squid in baking pan with a little olive oil in the bottom. Cover with cooked tomatoes and bake about 15 minutes. Season with salt and pepper. Serves 4.

Squid Piquant

3	pounds small squid	2	tablespoons bread
2	cloves garlic		crumbs
½	cup olive oil	2	tablespoons butter
1	small hot pepper	1	tablespoon parsley,
salt			chopped
		lemon wedges	

Clean, skin, and thoroughly wash squid. Sauté garlic in olive oil until lightly browned. Add the squid, small hot pepper, and a sprinkling of salt, and cook over a high flame about 5 minutes or until the squid are tender. Discard the garlic and pepper, stir in bread crumbs, butter, and parsley, and cook, stirring 2 minutes longer. Serve with lemon wedges. Serves 4.

Tentacle Stew

2	pounds squid, cleaned	1	clove garlic, minced
	(or 2 pounds tentacles)	2	cups canned tomato
½	pound ham, cut in		sauce
	½-inch cubes	10	drops Tabasco sauce
1	medium red onion,	1	cup water
	diced	½	teaspoon oregano
1	green pepper, diced	1	teaspoon curry powder

Heat a small stock pot and add the ham, heating it until about half the fat fries out. Add the onion, green pepper, and garlic, and cook, covered, until they are soft. Add the tomato sauce, seasonings, and water and simmer 15 minutes in the covered pot. Cut both squid and tentacles into bite-sized pieces, and add to the pot. Simmer no longer than 5 minutes; do not overcook. Serves 6.

SURF CLAM (MUSCLE)

A good recipe for baked "beach scallops," as the muscle of the surf clam is called, is to wash 1½ pounds of them in clam juice, place them in a pan with ½ cup of dry white wine, ¼ tablespoon salt, 1 tablespoon minced onions, 4 drops Tabasco, and a dash of cayenne pepper. Bring this mixture to a boil, cover, and simmer 10 minutes. Drain and save 1 cup of the broth. In the same pan, melt fresh salted butter, blend in 3 tablespoons flour, and then add the broth and ½ cup heavy cream. Stir constantly, and after mixture is thickened, add 1 cup grated sharp cheddar cheese, and then the "scallops." Put it all in a casserole, sprinkle the top with ½ cup of dark bread crumbs, and bake at 400° for 10 minutes. Bon appétit! Serves 4.

PERIWINKLES AND LIMPETS

Periwinkles and limpets may be boiled or steamed, as we've seen. Boil them in their shells, extract with a pin or strong toothpick and swallow immediately, either before or after dipping in brown butter. Some hardy souls hammer the end of the winkle and suck the snail out of the other end. You can also fry them, after boiling, in butter, bacon grease, or in the same batter as for mussels.

Glossary

Abdomen. The posterior part of the body of invertebrates, if the body is divided into distinct regions.

Aboral. Opposite the end or side of radially symmetrical animals, such as anemones, on which the mouth is located.

Adductor Muscle. In bivalve mollusks, a large muscle that pulls the valves of the shell together.

Alternation of Generations. In the life cycle, alternation between a phase that reproduces sexually and one that reproduces asexually.

Ambient. The same as the surrounding or prevailing environment (such as ambient temperature).

Antenna (plural antennae). In arthropods, one of a pair of jointed sensory appendages on the head.

Anterior. At or near the front end of the body.

Aristotle's lantern. A group of five teeth and some accessory structures associated with the mouths of sea urchins and sand dollars, used for breaking up food.

Article. A unit of an arthropod's appendage.

Artifact. A usually simple object, such as a tool or an ornament, which shows human workmanship or modification.

Avicularium (plural avicularia). In bryozoans, a type of individual that has two jaws and looks like a bird's beak.

Axial. Along the midline of the body or of some other structure.

Benthos (benthic). Collectively, all animals and plants living in or on bottom substrata in aquatic habitats.

Biome. Worldwide complex of communities characterized by the prevailing climatic and soil conditions.

Biota. The flora and fauna of a region.

Brackish. Somewhat salty; a combination of fresh and salt water.

Bud. An outgrowth of an organism that differentiates asexually into a new individual.

Budding. Type of asexual reproduction involving the appearance of new animals as outgrowths from an older individual, and their subsequent development into independent organisms or into colonies, depending on the species.

Byssus. In bivalve mollusks, organic material, generally in the form of threads, secreted by a gland at the base of the foot and used for attachment to the substratum.

Calcareous. Composed of calcium carbonate; limy; chalky.

Carapace. In crustaceans, a hard portion of the exoskeleton that covers the head and thorax.

Carnivorous. Eating other animals or the flesh of animals.

Cerata. In sea slugs, fleshy projections of the upper surface, each of which usually has a branch of the digestive tract in it.

Cilia (singular cilium). Vibratile, microscopic, hairlike projections of cells, important in locomotion, in creating water currents, and in other functions (structurally the same as flagella).

Colonial. A group of individuals of the same species aggregated and sometimes structurally connected.

Commensalism. A type of association between two species in which one (the commensal) lives on, in, or with the other, obtaining some benefit from the relationship, but neither harming nor benefiting its host appreciably.

Ctene. In a ctenophore, one of the paddlelike aggregations ("combs") of large cilia that propel the animal.

Ctenidium. In mollusks, a "true" gill, usually resembling a comb or feather (often lacking, or replaced by, other structures having a respiratory function).

Cypris. In barnacles, the larval stage that succeeds the nauplius and metamorphoses into the adult. It has six pairs of thoracic appendages and a bivalved shell.

Debris. The remains of fragmented organisms, rocks, or other materials.

Detritus. Finely divided organic matter derived from the disintegration of animals and plants.

Dorsal. Referring to the back or upper surface of the body.

Ecosystem. The complex interaction of a community and its environment, functioning as an ecological unit in nature.

Ecto-. A prefix referring to something that is external (for example, an ectoparasite).

Effluent. Waste material discharged into the environment, especially when it is a pollutant.

Endo-. A prefix referring to something that is internal.

Exoskeleton. An external skeleton, as in Crustacea and in other arthropods.

Exotic. Pertaining to any non-native introduced species.

Flotsam. Floating debris of all sizes and kinds.

Globose: Something spherical or rounded with a globular form.

Gonophore. In some coelenterates (especially hydroids), a reproductive polyp in which the medusa stage (or an abortive counterpart of the medusa) is produced.

Groin. A rigid structure built out from a shore to influence the effects of the moving water.

Holdfast. In seaweeds, an anchoring attachment at the base of the plant.

Host. An organism that provides a home—in its burrow, or on or within itself—for another species.

Jetsam. The part of a ship, its equipment, or its cargo which is cast overboard to lighten the load, and which sinks or is washed ashore.

Jetty. A synonym for groin; a landing wharf or pier.

Lateral. At the side; to one side of the midline.

Littoral. Roughly, the shoreline from the level of the highest to at least the level of the lowest tide.

Lophophore. In phoronids, bryozoans, and brachiopods, a circular or horseshoe-shaped ridge that bears ciliated tentacles used in feeding and respiration.

Madreporite. A perforated calcereous plate ("sieve plate") on the aboral surface of sea stars and sea urchins that permits water to enter the water-vascular (used for locomotion) system.

Mantle. In mollusks, an outer sheet of tissue that secretes the shell and also encloses the cavity within which the true gills (if present) are located.

Median. Referring to the midline of the body or of some structure.

Medusa. A jellyfish.

Molt. Every molt is a periodic shedding of the exoskeleton permitting an increase in size.

Morphological. The form or structure of an organism considered as a whole, or at least in its gross aspects.

Mutualism. A type of association between two species that is beneficial to both.

Nauplius. The first larval stage of many aquatic crustaceans, characterized by three pairs of appendages corresponding to the antennules, antennae, and mandibles of the adult.

Narcotize. To soothe a subject to unconsciousness or unawareness with a narcotizing agent.

Neap tides. Tides during the monthly cycle with the lowest highs and the highest lows; tides of low amplitude.

Niche. The unique position of an organism in the ecological scheme of things; its role in the food chain; its environmental requirements; and so on.

Notochord. In the vertebrates and other chordates, a firm, elastic rod, composed of cells and lying between the digestive tract and the dorsal nerve cord (it may not persist to the adult stage of the animal).

Operculum. A "trap door," such as the one the Snail uses to close its shell after the animal withdraws inside.

Oral. Referring to the mouth, or to the end or side of the body on which the mouth is located.

Osculum. In sponges, an opening through which water passes out of the body.

Ossicle. In echinoderms, a small calcareous plate or spine.

Pallets. Calcereous, featherlike structures secreted by the mantle of shipworms (bivalve mollusks burrowing in wood), used for closing the opening of the burrow.

Palp. Fleshy cylindrical or tapered projection, segmented or unsegmented, usually sensory, attached at the anterior (front) end of polychaetes and arthropods.

Parapodium (plural parapodia). In polychaet annelids, a fleshy flap of tissue on each side of most segments (the bristles are set into the parapodia); in some sea slugs, a winglike flap on each side of the body.

Parasite. An organism that lives on or in another organism, from which it obtains its nourishment.

Pedicellaria (plural Pedicellariae). In sea stars and sea urchins, a small, pincerlike structure on the body surface.

Pelagic. Pertaining to the open waters of seas (or of lakes), or to the organisms that inhabit these waters; applied to organisms, it means living in open waters, not anchored.

Periostracum. In mollusks, the organic material, often fibrous, on the outside of the shell.

Phytoplankton. Microscopic on up to very small plants suspended in aquatic habitats.

Pinnate. Branched in a featherlike pattern.

Plankton. The organisms, mostly small, which are suspended in the water and either drift with the currents or swim weakly.

Planula. In coelenterates, a ciliated plate-like larva developing from the fertilized egg.

Pleopod. In crustaceans, an abdominal appendage, used for swimming, respiration, holding egg clusters, and other functions.

Polyp. In coelenterates, an individual (in colonial types, it may serve only for feeding or it may be specialized for reproduction or some other function).

Polypide. In bryozoans, an individual member of a colony (a polypide together with the zooecium it secretes forms a zooid).

Posterior. At or near the hind end of the body.

Predacious. The practice of killing and eating another animal.

Proboscis. An extensile organ used in feeding.

Radial symmetry. A type of symmetry in which the structures of the body are arranged around a central longitudinal axis, so that the animal can be divided into equal halves by planes passing through this oral–aboral axis (as in jellyfishes, sea stars, and sea urchins).

Radula. In chitons and gastropods, a ribbonlike band of minute teeth that can be protruded through the mouth and used for scraping; sometimes modified into a venom-injecting apparatus.

Rhinophores. In sea slugs, a pair of tentacles, often elaborate, on the upper surface of the head.

Riprap. A foundation or a sustaining wall of boulders, or the like, put together in deep water or on an embankment slope to prevent erosion.

Rostrum. In crustaceans, a forward prolongation of the carapace.

Salt pond. A small, almost enclosed, more or less bowl-shaped coastal body of standing salt water.

Scud. A colloquial name for very common amphipods belonging to the genus *Gammerus*.

Sessile. Fixed tightly to the substratum and ordinarily not capable of moving.

Siliceous. Composed of, or containing silica.

Spat. Newly attached juvenile oysters.

Spicules. Small calcareous or siliceous structures that stiffen the body or parts of it in some animals (such as sponges).

Spring tides. Tides during the monthly cycle with the highest highs and the lowest lows; tides of greatest amplitude because the moon and the sun are on the same side of the earth.

Statocyst. An organ of balance, in which a small crystalline mass makes contact directly or indirectly with sensory cells.

Stolon. A "runner," that creeps over or through the substratum, from which new individuals (as in some hydroids, hydrozoans, and ascidians) are budded.

Substrate (plural, substrates). A substance that is acted upon, as by an enzyme.

Substratum (plural, substrata). The base of support on which an organism lives.

Symbiosis. A constant association between two species of organisms (includes parasitism, mutualism, and commensalism).

Symmetry. Balanced proportions; correspondence in size, shape, and relative position of parts on opposite sides of a body. The opposite of symmetry is asymmetry.

Systematics. Study of the diversity and relationships of organisms.

Taxonomy. Theory and practice of naming and classifying organisms.

Telson. The terminal segment ("tail") of a crustacean's abdomen.

Test. Protective shell or exoskeleton or both, composed of sand grains, debris, calcium carbonate, or other material.

Thorax. In crustaceans and other arthropods, the middle portion of the body, between the head and the abdomen.

Trochophore. The first larval stage of some mollusks, annelids, and related groups, generally more or less ovoid in shape, and with an apical tuft of cilia at the anterior end and bands of cilia encircling the body.

Tube feet. In echinoderms, extensile projections, sometimes with cuplike tips, used for locomotion and feeding.

Umbone (or Umbo). In bivalve mollusks, the oldest part of each valve, near the hinge, often elevated or somewhat beaklike.

Veliger. A larval stage of mollusks, succeeding the trochophore and eventually metamorphosing into the adult, with ciliated lobes for swimming and usually a shell.

Velum. In some jellyfishes, a circular membrane extending inward from the margin of the bell.

Ventral. Referring to the underside of the body.

Vermiform. Wormlike.

Vibraculum. In bryozoans, an individual modified into a slender, vibratile projection that apparently helps in warding off unwelcome visitors.

Zooecium. In bryozoans, the individual covering or chamber within which each animal (zooid) lives.

Zooplankton. Microscopic to very small animals, as well as developmental stages of larger animals, suspended in aquatic habitats.

Bibliography

The Biology of Marine Invertebrates

Amos, W. H. *The Life of the Seashore.* New York: McGraw-Hill, 1966.

Barnes, R. D. *Invertebrate Zoology*, 4th ed. Philadelphia: W. B. Saunders, 1980.

Bayre, R. M., and H. B. Owre. *The Free-Living Lower Invertebrates.* New York: Macmillan, 1968.

Brown, F. A., Jr. *Selected Invertebrate Types.* New York: John Wiley, 1950.

Gosner, K. L. *Guide to Identification of Marine and Estuarine Invertebrates: Cape Hatteras to the Bay of Fundy.* New York: Wiley-Interscience, 1971.

Hardy, A. C. *The Open Sea.* Boston: Houghton Mifflin, 1956.

Hyman, L. H. *The Invertebrates*, Vols. I–VI. New York: McGraw-Hill, 1940–1967.

Jaeger, E. C. *A Source-Book of Biological Names and Terms*, 3rd ed. Springfield, Mass.: Charles C. Thomas, 1972.

Lippson, J. L., and R. L. Lippson. *Life in the Chesapeake Bay.* Baltimore: Johns Hopkins University Press, 1984.

Miner, R. W. *The Field Book of Sea Shore Life.* New York: G. P. Putnam's Sons, 1950.

Nicol, J. A. C. *The Biology of Marine Animals.* New York: Pitman, 1960.

Pilkey, O. H., Jr., W. J. Neal, O. H. Pilkey, Sr., and S. R. Riggs. *From Currituck to Calabash.* North Carolina Science & Technology Research Center, Research Triangle Park, NC 27709.

Pratt, H. S. *Manual of the Common Invertebrate Animals* New York: P. Blakiston's Son, 1945.

Redfield, A. C. *Ontogeny of a Salt Marsh Estuary. Science* 147 (3635), January 1, 1965.

Russell-Hunter, W. D. *A Life of Invertebrates.* New York: Macmillan, 1979.

Southward, A. J. *Life on the Seashore.* Cambridge: Harvard University Press, 1967.

Yonge, C. M. *The Sea Shore.* London: William Collins, 1949.

Marine Invertebrates of the North Atlantic Coastal Waters

Abbott, R. T. *Seashells of North America.* Golden Field Guide. New York: Golden Press, 1968.

Arndt, C. H. Some insects of the between-tides zone. *Proceedings of the Indiana Academy of Science,* 12 (1914), 323–333.

Barnes, R. D., and B. M. Barnes. The ecology of spiders of maritime drift lines. *Ecology,* 35(1) (1954), 25–35.

Bliss, D. E. *Shrimps, Lobsters, and Crabs.* New York: Piscataway Press, 1982.

Campbell, R. Report on the shellfish survey of Block Island. Rhode Island Division of Fish and Game, Leaflet 5.

Coe, W. R. Biology of the nemerteans of the Atlantic Coast of North America. *Transactions of the Connecticut Academy of Arts and Sciences,* 35 (1943), 129–328.

DeLaubenfels, M. W. The sponges of Woods Hole and adjacent waters. *Bulletin of the Museum of Comparative Zoology,* Harvard University, 103(1) (1949), 1–55.

Emerson, W. K., and M. K. Jacobson. *The American Museum of Natural History Guide to Shells.* New York: Alfred A. Knopf, 1976.

Field, L. R. Sea anemones and corals of Beaufort, North Carolina. *Bulletin of the Duke University Marine Station* 5 (1949), 1–39.

Fraser, C. M. *Hydroids of the Atlantic Coast of North America.* Toronto: University of Toronto Press, 1944.

Galtsoff, P. S. The American Oyster *Crassostrea virginica* Gmelin. *Fishery Bulletin of the U.S. Fish and Wildlife Service.* 64 (1964), 1–480.

Gosner, K. L. *A Field Guide to the Atlantic Seashore.* Boston: Houghton Mifflin, 1979.

Hartman, W. D. Natural history of the sponges of southern New England. *Bulletin of the Peabody Museum of Natural History*, 12 (1958), 1–155.

Kirby-Smith, W. W., and I. E. Gray. A Checklist of Common Marine Animals of Beaufort, North Carolina. Duke University Laboratory Reference Museum, Beaufort, NC.

Knowlton, R. E. Preliminary Checklist of Maine Marine Invertebrates. *Research Institute, Gulf of Maine*, 1 (1971), 1–11.

Kunkel, B. W. The Arthrostraca of Connecticut. *Connecticut Geology and Natural History Survey*, 26 (1918), 1–261.

Morris, P. A. *A Field Guide to the Shells of Our Atlantic and Gulf Coasts*, 3rd ed. Boston: Houghton Mifflin, 1973.

Osburn, B. C. The Bryozoa of the Woods Hole Region. *Bulletin of the U.S. Bureau of Fisheries*, 30 (1912), 205–266.

Pettibone, M. H. Marine polychaete worms of New England, Parts I and II. *Bulletin of the U.S. National Museum*, 227 (1963), 1–356.

Plough, H. H. *Sea Squirts of the Atlantic Continental Shelf from Maine to Texas*. Baltimore: Johns Hopkins University Press, 1978.

Prudden, T. M. *About Lobsters*. Freeport, Me.: Bond Wheelwright, 1962.

Robbins, S. F. At the edge of the tide: Anurida, the tide pool insect. *Narragansett Naturalist*, 11(1) (Dec. 1969), 38–39.

Schmidt, W. L. *Crustaceans*. Ann Arbor: University of Michigan Press, 1965.

Singletary, R. L. Tide pools, nature's marine aquaria. *International Oceanographic Foundation* 18(1) (1972), 2–9.

Smith, R. I., ed. Keys to the Marine Invertebrates of the Woods Hole Region. Contribution 11, Systematics-Ecology Program, Marine Biological Laboratory, Woods Hole, Mass., 1964.

Van Name, W. G. The North and South American Ascidians. *Bulletin of the American Museum of Natural History*, 84 (1945); 1–476.

Wass, M. L. Check list of the marine invertebrates of Virginia. Virginia Institute of Marine Science. *Special Scientific Report*, 24 (1963), 1–56.

Wells, H. W., M. J. Wells, and I. E. Gray. Marine Sponges of North Carolina. *Journal of the Elisha Mitchell Scientific Society*, 76 (1960), 200–245.

Zinn, D. J. *Tethys (Aplysia) Willcoxi* in Narragansett Bay and Other Rhode Island Waters. *The Nautilus*, 64(2) (1950), 40–47.

———. Marine Mollusks of Cape Cod. Brewster, Mass.: Cape Cod Museum of Natural History, 1984.

Seaweed

Arnold, A. F. *The Sea-Beach at Ebb-Tide*. New York: Dover, 1968.

Dawes, C. J. *Marine Botany*. New York: John Wiley, 1981.

Dawson, E. Y. *Marine Botany: An Introduction*. New York: Holt, Rinehart and Winston, 1966.

———. *How to Know the Seaweeds*. Dubuque, Iowa: Wm. C. Brown, 1956.

Kingsbury, J. M. *Seaweeds of Cape Cod and the Islands*. Chatham, Mass.: Chatham Press, 1969.

Petry, L. C., and M. G. Norman. *A Beachcomber's Botany*. Chatham, Mass.: Chatham Press, 1975.

Taylor, W. R. *Marine Algae of the Northeastern Coast of North America*. Ann Arbor: University of Michigan Press, 1962.

Recipes

Angier, B. *Gourmet Cooking for Free*. New York: Stackpole, 1970.

Boulenger, E. G. *A Naturalist at the Dinner Table*. London: Gerald Duckworth, 1927.

Davidson, A. *North Atlantic Seafood*. New York: The Viking Press, 1980.

Fish and Seafoods Cookbook. New York: Better Homes and Gardens Books, 1971.

Gibbons, E. *Stalking the Blue-Eyed Scallop.* New York: David McKay, 1964.

Gourmet Magazine, 777 3rd Avenue, New York, N.Y. 10017.

Gowanloch, J. N. Fishes and fishing in Louisiana. New Orleans: State of Louisiana Department of Conservation Bulletin 23, 1933.

Hardigree, P. A. The Free Food Seafood Book. Harrisburg, Pa.: Stackpole, 1977.

Hunt, P. *Cape Cod Cookbook.* New York: Gramercy, 1962.

Madlener, J. C. *The Seavegetable Book.* New York: Clarkson N. Potter, 1977.

Milaradovich, M. *The Art of Fish Cookery.* New York: Doubleday, 1970.

Miller, G. B. *The Thousand-Recipe Chinese Cookbook.* New York: Athenaeum Press, 1966.

Reardon, J., and R. Ebbling. *Oysters.* Orleans, Mass.: Parnassus Imprints, 1984.

Spitzbergen, J. M. *Strange Seafood Recipes.* Beaufort, N.C.: Hampton Mariners Museums, 1982.

Tracy, M. *The Shellfish Cookbook.* New York: Bobbs-Merrill, 1965.

Index

A

Abbott, R. Tucker, 29
Acadian subprovince, 20
Acalephae, 67
Acorn (rock) barnacles, 16, 98, 99, 100, 101
Acorn worm, Hemichordata, 76, 78–79
aeolids, 189
Agardh's Red Weed, *Agardheilla tenera*, 42
Agassiz, Louis, 59, 99, 141
algae, 40
    brown, *Phaeophyta*, 40
    green, *Chlorophyta*, 40
    red. *Rhodophyta*, 40
American Indians, 178
Amos, William, 194
Amphinera, 156
amphipods, 129, 131
Angel wings, 172
Anomiidae, 161
arachnids, 136
archiannelids, 95
argillites, 15
argonauts, 195
Aristotle, 58, 152
Aristotle's Lantern, 142, 149
arthropod, 98, 102, 124, 134
Athenaeus, 187

B

Ballanoid-Thallophyte Biome, 21
Bamboo worm, *Clymenella*, 94
Banded weeds, *Ceramium*, 42
barnacles, 98–101, 108, 136, 153
    Balanomorpha, 98
    goose-necked, 98, 101
    Lepadomorpha, 98

Gonionemus murbachii, 59
Gonyaulix, 32
gorgonia, 69
Gotto, R. V., 95
Graceful red weed, Gracilaria foliifera, 42
granites, 15
graphites, 15
Green crab, Carcinides maenas, 110–111, illus. 110
Green fleece, codium fragile, 41
greenhead flies, 15
gribbles, 16
Gulfweed, Sargassum, 15, 41, 84
"gwean," 188

H

hard clam, 178
hardshell clam, 178
Haustorius, 131
Hermit crab, Pagurus pollicaris, 74, 95, 105–109, illus. 106
Herrick, F. H., 120
Heteronereis, 90
Historia Animalium, 58
Hollow green weeds, Enteromorpha, 40
Holothuroideans (also see Sea cucumber)
    Bêche-de-Mer, 147
    milky cucumber, Chiridota laevis, 147
    orange-footed cucumber, Cucumaria frondosa, 147
    Psolus fabricii, 147
    rat-tailed cucumber, Caudina arenata, 147
    Stichopus, 147
Holy Ghost shell, 143
Horseshoe crab, Limulus polyphemus, 16, 98, 132–137, illus. 133
    Xiphosura, 135
"horse-winkle," 188
hydroids, 16, 22, 62, 114, 190
    snail fur, Hydractinia echinata, 62, illus. 63, 108
    tubularian, 63

I

Idotea, 74
intertidal zonation, 20–21

Irish moss, *Chondrus crispus*, 15, 22, 42, illus. 43
Ivory barnacles, 16

J

Janthuria, 26
Jellyfish, 56–61
    frilled, *Dactylometra quinquecirrha*, 17, 59, 60
    Gonionemus murbachii, 59
    Liriope scutigera, 59
    medusa, 56, 58
    Pelagia cyanella, 59
    Periphylla hyacinthina, 59
    pink, *Cyanea capillata*, 59, 60
    Portuguese man-of-war, 17, 59, 60
    sea nettle, *Scyphozoa*, 59, 60
    sea wasp, 59, 60
    stalked, *Haliclystus auricula*, 17, 59
    white (moon), *Aurelia aurita*, illus. 57, 59
Jingle shell, *Anomia aculeata*, 159–163
    Anomia simplex, 136, 160, illus. 161, 162
    Filibranchia, 161
Jonah crab (northern), *Cancer borealis*, 20, 112–113, illus. 111

K

Kelp
    edible, *Alaria*, 41
    horsetail, *Laminaria digitata*, 15, 16, 41, 84
Keyhole-urchin, 141
"King" crab, 115
Kitten paws, 161
Knotted wrack, *Ascophyllum nodosum*, 22, 41

L

Lacy red weed, *Euthora cristat*, 42
Lady crab, *Ovalipes ocellatus*, 105, 109–110
Laminaria, see Kelp
Lankester, E. Ray, 78
Laver, *Porphyra*, 41
Leucosolenia, 48, 50

Limpet, *Acmaea testitudinalis*, 22, 27, 153, 162
    keyhole, 116
Linck, Johannes, 152
Linnaeus, Carl (Carolus), 85, 178
Liriope scutigera, 59
little neck, 178
Lobster, *Homarus americanus*, 20, 28, 119, 120–123, illus. 121, 124
    "chicken," 123
    spiny, *Panulirus argus*, 121
Loosanoff, Victor, 166
Lovell, M. S., 187
Lug worm, *Arenicola*, 88, 94

M

MacGinnitie, G. E. and N., 116
Mackie, G. O., 59
Malacostraca, 124
Marine Biological Laboratory, Woods Hole, Mass., 162
Mason (gold-tooth) worm, *Pectinaria gouldis*, illus. 92, 94
McIntosh, W. C., 78
Medusa, 56, 58
Meiofauna, 43
Mermaid's toenails, 159
mesopsammon, 43
microfauna, 43, 44
microflora, 43, 44
Midlittoral zone, lower, 22
Midlittoral zone, upper, 22
Mills, E. L., 132
Mole crab, *Hippa talpoida*, 118
Monograph on the Sub-Class Cirripedia, 1851–1854, 98
Moon jelly, 17
Moon snail, 16, 106, 179
moon stones, 15
Moss animals, 16, 22, 82–85
    Aetea anguina, 84
    avicularia, 82
    Bowerbankia gracilis, 84
    Bugula turrita, 84, 85, 114
    Cryptosula pallasiana, illus. 83

Ricketts and Calvin, 90
Rock (acorn) barnacles, *Balanus balanoides*, 16, 98, illus. 99,
  100, 101
Rock crab, *Cancer irroratus*, 112, 113
Rockweed, *Fucus*, 15, 22, 41, 84, 150
rocky shores, 21–23
round clam, 178
Russell-Hunter, W. D., 77

S

"sabot," 188
salt marshes, 25
sand bug, 118
Sand dollar, 140–143, 148, 150
  northern, *Echinarachnius parma*, 141, illus. 142
  southern, *Mellita quinquiesperforata*, illus. 141
Sand flea, 15, 129
Sand hopper, *Orchestia agilis*, 15, 128–132, illus. 129
Sargassum, (Gulfweed), 15, 41, 84
sandstones, 15
Sausage weed, *Scytosiphon lomentaria*, 41
Scaleworm
  Harmathöe, 94
  Lepidonotus, 84
Scallop, 27, 153, 161
  bay, *Aequipecten irradians*, 26, 40, 162
  beach, 177
Schistosoma, 185
Schmitt, Waldo, 101
scuds, 22
scungili, 193
Scypha, 48, 49, 50
Sea anenome, 61, 108
  Edwardsia leidyi, 69
sea arrow (Flying Squid), *Ommastrephes illecebrosa*, 196
"sea beef," 159
sea biscuit, 144
Sea cucumber, *Thyone briareus*, 95, 140, 144–147, illus. 145
  Leptosynapta inhaerens, 144, 145, illus. 146, 147
  Leptosynapta roseola, 144
seafan, 54, 57
Sea gooseberries, *Pleurobrachia pileus*, 66, 67, 68

purple, *Arbacia punctulata*, 148–150, illus. 149
sea, 17, 95, 140

V

Venus clam (widgeon), *Pitar morrhuana*, 183
Venus girdle, *Cestus veneris*, 67
"vignot," 188
Virginia subprovince, 20
"verlin," 188

W

"wampum," 178
Whelk (conch), 16, 176, 191–195
  dog, 22, 101
  channeled, *Busycon canaliculatum*, 191, 193–194
  knobbed, *Busycon carica*, 191, illus. 192, 193–194
  waved, *Buccinium undatum*, 191–193
Widgeon (witch) grass, *Ruppia maritima*, 39
Wildlife Observer's Guidebook, The, 29
Wilson, H. V., 50
Wine weed, *Ahnfeltia plicata*, 42
wing shells, 172
wood borer, 171
Worm Runner's Digest, 74
Worms
  acorn, Hemichordata, 76, 78–79
  bamboo, *Clymenella*, 94
  breakthrower, Glycera, 94
  clam, *Nereis virens*, 16, 88–91, illus. 89, 92, 94, 95
  fan, *Hydroides, Potamilla, Sebella, Serpula, Spirorbis*, 94
  flat (Turbellaria), 72–74
    Bdelloura candida, illus. 73, 136
    Gnesioceros sargassicola, 73
    Leptoplana, 72
    Micropharynx, 74
    oyster "leech," 74
    Stylochus, 73
  fringed, *Cirratulus*, 94
  gold-tooth (mason), *Pectinaria gouldi*, illus. 92, 94
  lug, *Arenicola*, 88, 94
  Lumbrinereis, 94

About the Author

Donald Zinn is an internationally known zoologist and former chairman of the Department of Zoology at the University of Rhode Island. He has been president of the National Wildlife Federation, a member of a presidential advisory panel on Timber and the Environment, a member of the U.S. Army Corps of Engineers' Shoreline Erosion Advisory panel, and currently serves as director of the New England National Resources Center.

Dr. Zinn has published numerous papers in scientific journals and magazines. He is the author of *The Marine Mollusks of Cape Cod*, published by the Cape Cod Museum of Natural History. Dr. Zinn lives on Cape Cod, in Massachusetts.

Other Books of Interest from The Globe Pequot Press

Nature Guides
Behavior and Learning of Animal Babies
Birding for the Amateur Naturalist
Botany for All Ages
Nocturnal Naturalist
World of Birds

Travel Guides
Recommended Country Inns series
    Mid-Atlantic • New England • South
Bed & Breakfast in New England
Bed & Breakfast in the Mid-Atlantic
Daytrips, Getaway Weekends, and Vacations in New England
Daytrips, Getaway Weekends, and Vacations in the Mid-Atlantic
    States
Off the Beaten Path series
    Georgia • Maryland • North Carolina • New Jersey • Virginia
Guide to Martha's Vineyard
Guide to Nantucket

Outdoor Recreation
Short Nature Walks series
    Cape Cod • Long Island • Connecticut
Short Bike Rides series
    Eastern Pennsylvania • Cape Cod, Nantucket & the Vineyard
    Connecticut • Greater Boston and Central Massachusetts
    Long Island • New Jersey • Rhode Island • Washington, D.C.

These and other nature, travel, and outdoor recreation books are available in bookstores or direct from the publisher. For a free catalogue, write The Globe Pequot Press, Box Q, Chester, CT 06412, or call 1-800-243-0495. In Connecticut, call 1-800-962-0973.